RUNNING A CHARITY

A Canadian Legal Guide

Revised and updated edition

Adam Aptowitzer LL.B

civil sector press

Running A Charity — A Canadian Legal Guide

Notice to Readers

Laws are constantly changing. Every effort is made to keep this publication and its companion website correct at the date of publication and as current as possible. However, the author, the publisher, and the vendor make neither representation nor warranties regarding the outcome of the use to which the information in this book is put and are not assuming any liability for any claims, losses, or damages arising out of the use of this book or its companion website. The reader should not rely on this book or its publisher for any professional advice. All information is subject to change without notice.

For current information and advice on your specific circumstances please contact a professional with expertise in the subject matter.

Drache Aptowitzer LLP lawyers can be contacted through www.drache.ca.

ISBN 9781927375525
Library and Archives Canada Cataloguing in Publication
Title: Running a charity : a Canadian legal guide / Adam Aptowitzer.
Other titles: Starting and maintaining a charity in Canada
Names: Aptowitzer, Adam, 1975- author.
Description: Second edition. | Includes index. | Originally published as Starting and maintaining a charity in Canada by Civil Sector Press, Toronto, 2014.
Identifiers: Canadiana (print) 20190205520 | Canadiana (ebook) 20190205539 | ISBN 9781927375525 (softcover) | ISBN 9781927375532 (Kindle) | ISBN 9781927375549 (EPUB)
Subjects: LCSH: Nonprofit organizations — Law and legislation — Canada. | LCSH: Nonprofit organizations —
Taxation — Law and legislation — Canada. | LCSH: Nonprofit organizations — Canada — Finance. | LCSH:
Charity laws and legislation — Canada. | LCSH: Charities — Taxation — Law and legislation — Canada. |
LCSH: Charities — Canada — Finance.
Classification: LCC KE1373 .A78 2019 | LCC KF1388 .A86 2019 kfmod | DDC 346.71/064 — dc23

Running A Charity — A Canadian Legal Guide

Publisher: Civil Sector Press
Canada
Box 86, Station C, Toronto, Ontario, M6J 3M7 Canada
Telephone: 416.267.1287
www.charityinfo.ca

United States of America
2626 Glenway Ave, Cincinnati, OH 45204 USA
Telephone: 513.471.6622

Editor: Jim Hilborn
Cover and interior book design and production: Cranberryink

To my parents Isaac and Naomi Aptowitzer.
Because (the law of) charity begins at home.

And to my wife Elana
For everything else.

About the author

Adam Aptowitzer is a tax lawyer with special expertise in the law as it pertains to charities, not-for-profit organizations, and other non-taxable entities anywhere in Canada. His practice involves tax litigation for private taxpayers and charities and he has represented clients at the Tax Court of Canada, the Federal Court of Appeal and the Supreme Court of Canada.

Adam's practice is diverse and includes (amongst other areas) high level tax planning for charities engaged in business activities, operating overseas, corporate governance and gift planning. He also works with international organizations seeking to work in Canada and with Canadian organizations operating abroad.

He also contributes to the public policy debate through academic papers and testimony to government committees. He regularly publishes in several journals, including the Canadian Taxpayer and the Not for Profit News. Adam has been recognized as among the premier charity law lawyers in Canada by the Canadian Lexpert® Legal Directory. And his firm, Drache Aptowitzer LLP, has been named one of the top ten tax law firms in the country.

In addition to his legal practice, Adam is an Associate Professor of Law at the University of Ottawa and has been called to the Bars of both Ontario and Alberta.

Table of Contents

PART I

Starting a Charity

———————

PART II

Maintaining a Charity

——————

PART III

Death of a Charity

Preface

In 1977, I wrote a book dealing with the taxation of charities — the first of its kind (as far as I know) to be published in Canada. That book which had a target audience of lawyers and accountants (the concept of professional fundraisers was in its infancy) was 148 pages and included every Income Tax Act provision, and Revenue Canada (as it was then) document about charities.

Today, the successor to that slim volume encompasses ten loose-leaf volumes and constitutes a comprehensive set of materials for the professional advisor but is not of much use to the average charity volunteer or even a board member.

Thus, the publication of *Running A Charity — A Canadian Legal Guide* by my long-time colleague Adam Aptowitzer fills a significant need providing a comprehensive overview of the relevant legal issues for those non-experts involved in charities. This audience includes volunteers at all levels and of course directors or trustees.

Aptowitzer is well qualified to write this book as his practice has emphasized the setting up of charities, their ongoing operations and occasionally, their demise. He has a wide experience in dealing with (or occasionally fighting with) the Canada Revenue Agency over issues relating to charities and thus writes from extensive first-hand experience. Also, unlike my original book which limited itself to tax issues, this book ranges far beyond the provisions of the *Income Tax Act*, covering key federal and provincial corporate issues.

Aptowitzer would be the first to acknowledge that even a complete mastery of this material will not make one an expert. But this book does give one an overview of the astonishing number of issues which a charitable board of directors might face over any given period of time.

In my view, the importance of this book is that it gives those who do not spend day in and day out working in charity law a heads up on issues which he or she may face as a board member, volunteer, or staff person. What is particularly valuable is not only that the arrangement and the writing makes the issues accessible, but also that the book allows the reader to formulate the appropriate questions for professional advisers, thereby setting the stage for getting germane answers.

For example, the impact of the GST (or HST in some provinces) is so arcane that even the vast majority of professional advisers are often leery of opining on the issue. In Chapter 9, however, Aptowitzer summarizes the rules so that a board member can be alert to situations where a decision may have an impact of GST liability. This prepares the reader to ask an accountant or lawyer specific questions while armed with an overview of the rules.

I would anticipate that this book will become a sort of Bible for those who lead and administer charities and might usefully be given to people who are newly involved with any nonprofit organization as part of an introduction to their duties and obligations.

I highly recommend it.

Arthur B. C. Drache CM, QC

Introduction

With great privilege comes great regulation.

Historically, many of the responsibilities that are currently performed by government were the responsibility of groups of people — usually religious — who worked to help their neighbours. In modern times these groups of people have become more highly organized and specialized. Governments have learned to work with these groups by sharing responsibility for some areas of charity — such as health care and education – and by creating tax incentives for those who donate to charity.

Unfortunately, with the special privileges accorded charities come great regulation designed to ensure that these privileges are not abused. Such rules are frustrating for the vast majority of people involved in charity who adhere to the innate instinct and principle of simply wishing to help their fellow neighbours.

This book is written for those people, and for the numerous directors, fundraisers, lay leaders, professionals and volunteers who work to help for the good of humankind. While there are many rules and regulations that affect charities, just as they affect all actors in society, charities must contend with an extra layer of regulation contained mostly within the *Income Tax Act*. Unfortunately, the *Income Tax Act* (and other laws) along with various regulations, schedules, interpretation bulletins, guidances and cases are simply inaccessible for the vast majority of charities. And so, this book is my attempt to help charities maintain compliance with the law while continuing their good work.

While the work in this book is mine, it could not have been completed without the aid of several colleagues. I would like to thank: Arthur Drache for his encouragement in undertaking this project and Alexandra Tzannidakis for her contributions on early drafts of some of the chapters; Eric Brown for his research on Chapter 4 and Jim Hilborn, and Mary Singleton of Civil Sector Press for bringing the book to fruition.

Finally, the Talmud tells us that the last in the list are those closest to our heart. I want to thank my wife Elana for her constant support in allowing me the time necessary to pursue this project and caring for Mia, Noa and Asher while I researched and wrote. To the extent that this book helps charities heal the sick, feed the hungry, clothe the naked, shelter the homeless, and educate the ignorant it is because of her.

Adam Aptowitzer
Ottawa, Ontario
2020

PART I

Starting
a Charity

———

1 | Fundamentals

People are often surprised that there are detailed and extensive laws governing the way we give charity and to whom we give it. In fact, there are laws on every aspect of charity, including the way charities are created, destroyed, registered or deregistered, and how they raise, spend, and keep money. The government's extensive regulation of charities can be traced back to the time when the state began to ensure that property intended for community use had special treatment. Regulation gained increasing momentum as the state became involved in what historically were charitable activities such as treating the sick. Adding to the reasons for regulation today, the government uses tax incentives to encourage the public to donate to charity. These all led to numerous rules to ensure the integrity of both the charities and the tax base. This chapter will survey the development of charity law in Canada to date and review some of the fundamentals of the administration of charities.

HISTORY OF THE LAW OF CHARITY IN ENGLAND

The history of Canadian charity law begins for all intents and purposes in England in 1601 when Queen Elizabeth I passed what is variously known as the *Statute of Uses* or the *Statute of Elizabeth*. The preamble to this Act — just a few lines, really — referred generically to certain purposes which might qualify as what has come to be known as charitable:

> The relief of the aged, impotent and poor people; the maintenance of sick and maimed soldiers and mariners, schools of learning, free schools and scholars in universities; the repair of bridges, ports, havens, causeways, churches, sea-banks and highways; the education and preferment of orphans; the relief, stock or maintenance of houses of correction; the marriages of poor maids, the supportation, aid and help of young tradesmen, handicraftsmen and persons decayed; the relief or redemption of prisoners or captives; and the aid or ease of any poor inhabitants concerning payment of fifteens, setting out of soldiers and other taxes.

For many years this preamble was used by the English courts as a guide in enforcing charitable bequests in Wills, with periodic expansions in its application and under-standing. In 1891, a case came before the Privy Council of the House of Lords in the United Kingdom which, while not a Canadian case, would become the major case defining modern charity law for Canada. In reorganizing the classification of charity law for the entire Commonwealth, the Council's Lord MacNaghten said:

> "Charity in its legal sense comprises four principle divisions: trusts for the relief of poverty; trusts for the advancement of education; trusts for the advancement of religion; and trusts for other purposes beneficial to the community, not falling under any of the previous heads."

These four categories became known as the "heads of charity." The meaning of the heads, particularly the last one, is discussed and interpreted by courts to this day. The list was not intended to be an exhaustive list of what qualified as charitable. Rather, new advancements in the definition of charity would evolve by analogy from items already considered charitable. At the same time, the 1601 preamble was not forgotten; anything which fell under the "spirit and intendment" of the original 1601 preamble would fall generically under one of the heads of charity. At this point, the main appli-cation of the Heads in Canada is in determining which purposes are charitable for income tax purposes.

Today, when an organization applies to the Canada Revenue Agency (CRA) for regis-tration as a charity, the government analyzes the organization's objectives to determine if a court has already found them to be charitable. If not, the CRA may still consider them charitable if there is a CRA policy recognizing these objects as charitable (again usually determined on the basis of analogy to previous cases). If the CRA refuses to register on the grounds that the proposed objects are not charitable, the proposed charity can appeal this determination up to the Supreme Court of Canada. A court can overturn the CRA's decision and declare the objects charitable. The same path can be taken in a situation where the CRA revokes or annuls a charity's registration.

HISTORY OF THE LAW OF CHARITY IN CANADA

Canada did not have an income tax until 1917, when funding the First World War made an income tax imperative. At the time, Parliament excluded certain wartime charities from paying tax on their income. In the 1930s, the government of William Lyon McKen-zie King proposed changes to the *Income War Tax Act* which would extend tax benefits to charities generally, and not just to those named specifically in the original law. The new rules also allowed ordinary Canadian taxpayers to deduct charitable donations from their income. This precipitated the first (and last) serious public discussion about the definition of "charity." Many Parliamentarians felt that to get around the rather intense dispute, the system would simply leave this definition to the courts.

After the passage of the *Income War Tax Act,* it still fell to the provincial courts to review and occasionally update the list of those aims considered charitable. (Of course, now the *provincial* court's decisions also had implications for the *federal* taxability of an organization). Following World War II, the special tax treatment of charitable organizations led to widespread abuses, in particular because of the deductibility of charitable donations from personal income. The abuse was facilitated in part by the fact that any group that held itself to be a charity could accept donations, resulting in special tax treatment for the donor without any real government oversight. As a result of these abuses, Parliament debated a system that would require charities to be registered in order to qualify for special tax treatment. The proposed registration system created a heated political situation when priests of the Catholic Church in Québec felt that their trustworthiness as clergy was being impugned. In their opinion, there was no reason to license any particular type of church organization.

Despite the political firestorm, the *Income Tax Act* was amended again in the 1960s to require charitable organizations to be registered in order to receive the twin benefits of tax-exempt income for themselves and tax-"deductible" donations for their donors. The registration system went live in 1967 with a total of 13,000 registered charities. Future inclusion in the registry was left to the newly-formed Charities Directorate of Revenue Canada (as the Canada Revenue Agency was then known). This task required the Directorate to apply the common law definition of charity to candidates for registration.

Upon Confederation, the power to determine what was, or was not, charitable fell exclusively to the Provincial Courts, a situation that still exists today. However, disputes over registration under the *Income Tax Act* (once the registration system was implemented) did not go to Provincial Courts, but rather went straight from Revenue Canada to the Federal Court of Appeal. So while technically, the Federal Court of Appeal does not have any jurisdiction to define what is or is not a charity, it does have authority to define what is or is not eligible for registration. Because this includes, by implication, determining what is charitable, the Federal Court of Appeal became the predominant court for resolving issues of charitable aims in Canada.

Predictably, the convoluted history of charity law in Canada has led to a convoluted situation for charities in operation today. As it stands, for a charity to achieve registration it must comply with the CRA's understanding of the definition of "charity," which is not necessarily the same as a given provincial definition, and it must also comply with any additional restrictions placed upon a charity by the *Income Tax Act*. If a dispute arises as to whether it is eligible for registration, it must appeal any decision of the CRA to the Federal Court of Appeal.

To further complicate the issue, some other areas affecting charities are exclusively provincial. For example, when dealing with legislation regarding fundraising or property taxes, a charity must comply with provincial understandings of what qualifies as charitable.

Navigating the maze of charity law in Canada can be extremely difficult, and professional advice is required to ensure that all perspectives on an issue have been considered.

WHAT CAN BE DONATED?

Anything can be freely given to a charity, be it money, gifts (such as clothing), or services (such as volunteer time.) However, while the *Income Tax Act* allows receipts to be issued for property, no receipts may be issued for the donation of services. The legal definition of property can be somewhat tedious, but essentially property is an item over which the owner has rights over it whether it is tangible or intangible. This is perhaps an obvious description when discussing something tangible such as land, a car, gold or a table, but it becomes more difficult when discussing "things" such as corporate shares or patents.

A service is effectively anything that is not property. Again, certain concepts are obvious. One would certainly expect a volunteer at a bake sale to be volunteering a service. However, the definition extends to professionals who offer their services to the charity. A lawyer, plumber, accountant, or painter who provides their professional services to the charity cannot receive a receipt for the value of those services, even though they would normally have received payment.

WHAT IS A GIFT?

In law, there are three elements that must occur for a gift to be valid they are:

1. A property. This implies either a tangible piece of property (such as furniture, a watch, or books) or the bundle of rights that allows control over an intangible piece of property (such as corporate shares, or intellectual property). In order to meet this test, it must be clear which property is being transferred.

2. A transference of ownership. This implies that the ownership of the item was clear in the first place and that its control was effectively transferred, both legally and practically. In some cases this is fairly easy to establish. For example, transference of ownership of a watch is clear one person had it then the other did. On the other hand, transference of some other items, usually intangible, relies on the completion of documents transferring ownership. For example, shares of publicly-traded corporations require the completion of legal documentation to transfer the shares from the name of one owner into the name of another. Finally, some objects have ownership transferred by way of constructive transfer. In making a gift of a car, one transfers the keys, which is not just a proxy for the car but actual control.

3. There must be the intention to give. This is usually clear from the transaction, but the most important element of this test is that there is no payment (in either money or barter) for the item being transferred.[1]

---

[1] While this is the technical requirement, the current law does allow for partial payment for a gift with the part not paid for being considered a gift and therefore receiptable.

4.   And finally, there must be acceptance of the gift. While this is often glossed over by most charities and assumed by most donors, the recipient of a gift can in fact refuse to accept it. This sometimes happens when a charity receives a gift from a politically unpalatable donor. In one famous example, Bette Midler donated a large sum of money to her alma mater, a religious girls' school, but the school refused the gift because it disapproved of the way she was living her life.

TAX FUNDAMENTALS

The *Income Tax Act* is an immensely complicated document comprising sections, subsections, paragraphs, subparagraphs, clauses and sub-clauses in thousands of pages, with cases and commentaries to help explain the law. Part of the reason for the complexity of the Act is that the government uses it to encourage certain behaviours and discourage others. For example, donating to charity is one of the behaviours the Act encourages. In order to understand how donations are encouraged one must first understand the basic structure of the Act.

Income vs. capital

When a gift is made to a charity, the taxes payable by the donor are not technically the charity's concern. Practically speaking, however, charities can hardly encourage donations when they do not understand the actual cost of those donations to the donors. In fact, charities that truly understand the cost of the donation can be more successful in raising funds — especially large donations. A successful charity understands that the taxes owing on donated items are a major practical concern.

Not surprisingly, the *Income Tax Act* taxes income. However, the term "income" is not a completely straightforward description of what it is actually taxed. For most individuals it includes salary, pensions, business earnings and other cash accumulated during the year. There are various rules for calculating the percentage of these earnings included in income for tax purposes. However, taxable income can also include the net amount of any gains from the "disposition" (i.e. the sale, giving away, or otherwise loss of ownership) of capital items. Effectively, a capital item is anything that produces revenue. For example, to a taxi driver that owns just one car the car is a capital property, but to a car salesman that same car is inventory because the car itself becomes revenue. Cars are just one example — in truth, just about any property can qualify as either capital property or inventory, including intellectual property and shares of a corporation. Unfortunately, the distinction is subjective, heavily dependent on the type of property and the use the owner makes of it.

In Canada, capital taxes are levied on the gain in value on the property during the time it was owned by the person disposing of it. When property loses value, no tax is paid. The law contains a variety of rules for calculating gain, depending on the type of property and the tax consequences that arise on the disposition of that property. The disposition (i.e. the sale, giving away, or otherwise losing ownership) of a capital item results in a capital gain if the property has increased in value during the period of ownership, taking into account any costs that went into owning the capital item. Under the *Income Tax Act*, only 50% of the gain is included in income for tax purposes. So, one is better off earning wealth through capital gains rather than through salary (for example). As noted earlier, items which are capital to some people are considered inventory for others. Someone who sells a capital property is only taxed on 50% of the gain, whereas a person who sells inventory is taxed on 100% of the profit.

Donations

In the context of charitable donations, when cash earned in a year is donated to charity it is nevertheless included in income for the year. If a capital good is donated to charity, the proceeds of the disposition are generally included in income, pending any special tax treatment in the Act. The donation tax credit or deduction is then applied later in the process. This is described in more detail in Chapter 3.

It may be impossible for a charity to know whether a particular item is being held as a capital item or as inventory by a particular donor, as this may not be obvious. However, charities should be aware that the consequences to the donor depend on how the property is held.

Deductions

Once all the income is added up, the *Income Tax Act* allows for certain deductions from income which are not considered taxable. The big one for most people is the RRSP deduction. If someone earned $100,000 and transferred $10,000 to their RRSP, only $90,000 of their income would be taxable. **Charitable donations by corporations (not individuals) are also treated as deductions from income**.

Once the net income (i.e. total income minus deductions) is determined, the various tax rates and income brackets are applied. The federal formula and most provincial and territorial formulas tax progressively. This means that the first bracket is taxed at a lower rate than the next bracket, and so on. Below is an example using the 2019 federal rates:

- 15% on the first $47,630 of taxable income

- 20.5% on the next $47,629 of taxable income (on the portion of taxable income over $47,630 up to $95,259)

- 26% on the next $52,408 of taxable income (on the portion of taxable income over $95,259 up to $147,667)

- 29% on the next $62,704 of taxable income (on the portion over $147,667 up to $210,371)

- 33% over $210,371

The same calculation that takes place federally also takes place provincially, although there may be a few extra deductions and the rates and brackets for the provinces are different than those for the federal government and from each other. A list of the various tax rates and brackets as of January 1, 2019 follows:

Table of provincial/territorial tax rates[2]

PROVINCES AND TERRITORIES	RATES
Newfoundland and Labrador	8.7% on the first $37,591 of taxable income, + 14.5% on the next $37,590, + 15.8% on the next $59,043, + 17.3% on the next $53,689, + 18.3% on the amount over $187,913
Prince Edward Island	9.8% on the first $31,984 of taxable income, + 13.8% on the next $31,985, + 16.7% on the amount over $63,969
Nova Scotia	8.79% on the first $29,590 of taxable income, + 14.95% on the next $29,590, + 16.67% on the next $33,820, + 17.5% on the next $57,000, + 21% on the amount over $150,000
New Brunswick	9.68% on the first $42,592 of taxable income, + 14.82% on the next $42,592, + 16.52% on the next $53,307, + 17.84% on the next $19,287, + 20.3% on the amount over $157,778
Quebec	Go to Income tax rates (Revenu Québec website: https://bit.ly/37WhG6t)
Ontario	5.05% on the first $43,906 of taxable income, + 9.15% on the next $43,907, + 11.16% on the next $62,187, + 12.16% on the next $70,000, + 13.16 % on the amount over $220,000
Manitoba	10.8% on the first $32,670 of taxable income, + 12.75% on the next $37,940, + 17.4% on the amount over $70,610
Saskatchewan	10.5% on the first $45,225 of taxable income, + 12.5% on the next $83,989, + 14.5% on the amount over $129,214

---

[2] Taken from http://www.cra-arc.gc.ca/tx/ndvdls/fq/txrts-eng.html

PROVINCES AND TERRITORIES	RATES
Alberta	10% on the first $131,220 of taxable income, + 12% on the next $26,244, + 13% on the next $52,488, + 14% on the next $104,976, + 15% on the amount over $314,928
British Columbia	5.06% on the first $40,707 of taxable income, + 7.7% on the next $40,709, + 10.5% on the next $12,060, + 12.29% on the next $20,030, + 14.7% on the next $40,394, + 16.8% on the amount over $153,900
Yukon	6.4% on the first $47,630 of taxable income, + 9% on the next $47,629, + 10.9% on the next $52,408, + 12.8% on the next $352,333, + 15% on the amount over $500,000
Northwest Territories	5.9% on the first $43,137 of taxable income, + 8.6% on the next $43,140, + 12.2% on the next $53,990, + 14.05% on the amount over $140,267
Nunavut	4% on the first $45,414 of taxable income, + 7% on the next $45,415, + 9% on the next $56,838, + 11.5% on the amount over $147,667

Credits

Once the taxpayer knows the gross amount of tax *payable* for a year, he or she can deduct any applicable tax credits. In other words, a tax credit directly reduces the amount payable, whereas a tax deduction simply reduces the amount of income upon which tax was calculated. Donations to charity by individuals result in tax credits. For example, if a taxpayer owes $10 in tax but is entitled to tax credits of $9, she will only be liable for a tax of $1. Thus, they can be very valuable to a donor who has tax owing to the government.

The calculation of tax credits resulting from donations is fairly simple. The federal government applies the lowest tax credit rate (i.e. 15%) on the first $200 of value and a higher rate on all amounts in excess of that. That rate is either 33% or 29% depending on the tax bracket of the individual. The intention is that the tax credit offsets the tax that would otherwise be payable on the dollar donated. This way, an individual does not pay tax on money given to charity. All the common law provinces follow a similar system, except that Alberta provides additional credits for the donation and several of the provinces still demand some amount of tax from a donor on funds that individual gives to a charity.

Many people think that donating a dollar to charity is donating a dollar that they otherwise would have paid in tax. "Better it should go to charity than the government" is a common refrain, but the truth is that any donation still requires some pain on the part of the donor. In British Colombia, for example, at the highest possible combined tax rates a donor would pay 49.80 cents in tax on a dollar earned, and would keep 51.20 cents. If that taxpayer decided to donate that dollar to charity he would basically be donating 51.20 cents, with the government(s) contributing the other 49.80 cents. At the highest bracket, the donor is still out 54 cents for every dollar donated.

Donations by corporations

Corporations can donate the same "things" as individuals, but their tax treatment differs. Donations by corporations do not generate tax credits, just deductions. The difference, as described above, is that a deduction reduces *only* the taxable income upon which tax is calculated, whereas a credit actually reduces the amount of tax payable. Given the choice, a donor would always prefer to receive a credit as opposed to a deduction.

Corporate donations to charity that also serve a business purpose can be deducted regardless of whether a charitable donation tax receipt has been issued. For example, a corporation that makes X-Ray machines may justify donating cash to the hospital for the business purpose of maintaining the hospital's good will. Determining whether the donation (or what percentage of it) qualifies as a business expense can be difficult and best left to a professional accountant. Ultimately though, it is in the corporation's best interests to have the charitable donation tax receipt; because if the CRA disagrees that the "donation" serves a business purpose, the corporation can always rely on the fact that it was deductible by virtue of being a charitable donation. Nevertheless, the charity would still be responsible for deducting from the amount of the receipt the total value of goods or services returned to the donor or to people not at arm's length from the donors.

In order to claim a charitable deduction, the corporation must receive a tax receipt from a registered Canadian charity. However, it is common knowledge that corporate expenses are generally deductible from the corporation's taxable income. Thus, some readers may wonder why a corporation needs to receive a receipt in order to properly make the deduction. The answer lies in the reason for making the donation.

A corporation can claim a business deduction if the donation can be justified as an *expense* that would have been necessary to earn income. For example, a neighbourhood business may feel compelled to give to a local cause where not doing so would engender bad will from the community for being stingy — thus affecting the bottom line.

If the donation cannot be justified as a business expense, the corporate donor will have a difficult time justifying the deduction. For this reason, it is common for corporate donors to request a receipt and avoid the possible problem of justifying the deduction.

Donations by individuals

The federal government collects taxes on its own behalf and personal taxes on behalf of all the provinces except Québec. In all of these jurisdictions, the governments provide tax credits equal to the lowest marginal rate on the first $200 of donations and at the highest rate on all donations after the first $200. Because our system levies income taxes based on increasing rates, the after-tax cost of donating more than $200 increases as overall income increases so the credit rate has to increase to offset the tax.

The tax rates are applied to the aggregate amount of the donor's receipts in a year. Thus, the rules above apply regardless of the item donated. At the end of this chapter a chart demonstrates the relative credits associated with a $1,200 donation. This should not be confused with the cost of donating a capital item, a calculation that requires several additional factors to be considered.

Limits on donations

It may surprise many Canadians to know that the Act places limits on the amount of income for which a donor can use a tax credit (or deduction) in a particular year. This amount is limited to 75% of the taxable income of the donor in a particular year, subject to certain exclusions. This limit does not apply to a donation made by will in the year of death, where a bequest by Will could not only offset 100% of the tax owing in the year of death but could be carried back to offset up to 100% of the tax owing in the previous year. There are certain other elements of making a donation in the year of death which are discussed in Chapter 5.

Carry-forwards

A tax credit can be used to offset tax owing in the year of the donation and any of the next five years. A donation of $1,000 in 2020 can offset taxes in 2020, 2021, 2022, 2023 or 2024, or any portion of taxes in any of those years, until the credit is depleted. Donation tax credits cannot be carried back to offset tax in a previous year (except in the case of a gift by Will).

Gifts by will

One legal requirement of a gift is actual delivery of the gift to the recipient. However, where a gift is made by will, such delivery is impossible until after the death of the person — sometimes well after. Under normal circumstances, the gift would not be complete until delivery is made. However, the law allows that where a gift is made by Will, it will be considered to have been made by the deceased in the few seconds preceding death, assuming of course that delivery occurs at some point after the death. In this way, the tax credits that are generated by the donation can be applied to the donor's year of death. This is particularly useful, as there is often a large tax bill owing on death.

The law allows for certain differences from a strict calculation perspective. As previously discussed, a donor is generally only entitled to offset 75% of their taxable income using donation tax credits in a given year. However, in the year of death (i.e. from January 1st until the date of the donor's death) the donor is entitled to offset up to 100% of their income, as filed by their executor. Any unused donation tax credits can be carried back one year, to the year preceding death, and be used to offset 100% of the tax debt owing in that year as well as the tax in the first three taxation years of the estate. One stipulation though is that the gift must be transferred (and accepted) by the qualified donee within three years of the death Obviously, if the return for the year preceding death has already been filed, then it will be necessary to file an adjustment request in order to claim the donation tax credits.

Provincial residency

As usual in tax matters, the various provinces add an additional layer of complexity to the calculation of taxes and, by extension, donation tax credits. Most provinces follow the same general pattern as the federal government. That is, donation tax credits on the first $200 of the donation are calculated based on the lowest tax rate of the province. Donations over and above the first $200 are given tax credits at a higher tax rate (often the highest of the province).

Below is a chart of the lowest and highest tax rates for the various provinces. The donation tax credit is calculated the same way for both the federal and provincial governments. The lesser of $200 or the amount of the donation is multiplied by the lowest tax rate in both the federal system and that of the donor's province of residence. If more than $200 was donated in a year, the calculation is $200 x (the combined lowest federal and provincial rates) + (the rest of the donation) x (the combined highest federal and provincial rates).

The following table provides examples of the differences that residency makes to the calculation of the gross tax amount for 2018 on donations of $1200. While this book focuses on the tax aspects of operating a charity, it should be noted that some provinces also have nonprofit licensing and reporting requirements outside of the tax regimes.

Province	Combined federal/provincial tax credit rate on first $200 donation	Tax credit	Combined federal/provincial tax credit rate on amounts over $200[5]	Tax credit on amount over $200	Total combined federal and provincial tax credit
Alberta[4]	25.00%	$50.00	54.00%	$540.00	$590.00
British Columbia	20.06%	$40.12	49.80%	$498.00	$538.12
Manitoba	25.8%	$51.60	50.4%	$504.00	$555.60
New Brunswick	24.68%	$49.36	50.95%	$509.50	$558.86
Newfoundland	23.70%	$47.40	51.3%	$513.00	$560.40
Northwest Territories	20.90%	$41.80	47.05%	$470.50	$512.30
Nova Scotia	23.79%	$47.58	54.00%	$540.00	$587.58
Nunavut	19.00%	$38.00	44.50%	$445.00	$483.00
Ontario[5]	20.05%	$40.10	44.16%	$441.60	$481.70
Prince Edward Island[6]	24.80%	$49.60	49.70%	$497.00	$546.60
Saskatchewan	25.50%	$51.00	47.50%	$475.00	$526.00
Yukon	21.40%	$42.80	45.8%	$458.00	$500.80

[3] For the sake of simplicity we assume the highest Federal tax bracket, but even if the individual was in the second highest bracket the credit rate would drop down to offset the tax owing in that federal bracket.

[4] The tax credit for donations over $200 more than offsets the taxes that would otherwise have been due.

[5] When the provincial surtaxes are taken into account, the offset at the highest marginal rates is somewhat higher.

[6] As PEI charges surtaxes when provincial tax exceeds $12,500, the effect of the offset is higher with income over approximately $99,000 (assuming a single individual with only the basic personal exemption).

2 | Charity Structure

The use of the term "charity registration" is well-known in Canada but few have ever stopped to think about what this means. Fundamentally, it means that in order to be registered as a charity, an entity must first exist that is capable of registration. In the same way a baby must be born before its birth can be registered, so too must the charity be created before it can become a *registered* charity.

This also implies that a charity can be created that is not registered as such. While these are relatively rare in Canada because unregistered charities do not get the same tax benefits as registered ones, it is technically possible. However, because most people intending to do good works do require the benefits of registration with the Canada Revenue Agency this book deals with the rules for obtaining and keeping *registered* charity status.

It is important to remember that the process by which an organization is created and the process by which it becomes registered are different and carried out through separate means. Registration as a charity is carried out *only* by the CRA while organizing *never* involves the CRA. There are several different forms under which an organization can be constituted, and incorporation can be accomplished either federally or provincially. This chapter will review the different forms of organization and outline some of the ongoing maintenance responsibilities that the different forms of organizations require.

UNINCORPORATED ASSOCIATION

The first and most basic way an association can be organized is simply as a group of people that get together to do good work. Typically, this involves friends or neighbours who identify a need and seek to address it through common action.

The rules by which such an organization may operate are entirely up to the group (so long as they do not contravene any laws). For example, they may involve everybody having a similar say in the running of the organization or it may be structured as a hierarchy. Voting can take place as the group decides, or not at all, and there may or may not be any terms for termination of membership in the group.

In order to obtain registration as a charity the group will have to produce some form of constituting document. This could have a variety of different names. It could be called a constitution, memorandum of association, or have some sort of religious nomenclature. What they all have in common are a name for the group, charitable objects, and a dissolution clause. The dissolution clause is critical for the CRA to register the organization as a charity. Typically it requires that on dissolution, the assets of the charity are distributed to qualified donees as that term is defined under the *Income Tax Act*. Organizations may also wish to include an amending clause in the constitution should they encounter any reason to amend the documents in the future. A sample constitution is available at **www.runningacharity.ca**.

While organizing as an association has its advantages, for example being easy and inexpensive, there are also certain disadvantages. First among them is the general lack of liability protection for the members of the group. That is to say that liability for unpaid bills or damages which may be caused in the course of the charity's operations become the personal obligations of the members. This is also true of legal obligations such as source deductions from employees. In fact, if the organization is ever revoked, the members of the group could become personally responsible for the revocation tax. Even though nobody *plans* to owe money to the government (or anyone else) we generally advise not to pursue registration as an unincorporated association because of the difficult personal consequences which may arise if the charity does run into financial difficulties.

One other disadvantage is the inherent lack of formality within an unincorporated group. The lack of bylaws and the lack of a governing law to govern the actions of such an operation may be seen as a plus, but in fact members of the group often do not know how to properly operate the group in the event that certain circumstances arise (such as termination of membership or a dispute over control of the organization). Consequently, if an unplanned for situation arises the organization may become ungovernable.

Unincorporated associations are also limited in other ways. For example, a private foundation cannot be set up as an unincorporated association. Furthermore, an unincorporated group cannot guarantee a loan or own real estate in its own name (with certain exceptions for religious organizations).

In circumstances where the charity knows for certain it will not be engaged in any type of actual operation and exists solely to dispense funds to other charities, then there may be some sense in using an unincorporated association. However, in the long run, and certainly for groups that propose to carry on actual fundraising operations and pursue charitable objects, an unincorporated association has inherent risks which can easily be avoided by pursuing incorporation as discussed below.

CHARITABLE TRUST

The Statute of Elizabeth was necessary because at the time, charitable trusts were created when an individual would, by Will, leave their assets for particular uses. In return, the state would accord them special treatment. A trust is effectively a relationship between people governing the use of property. A typical trust defines who legally owns property and who has the rights to benefit from that property. A charitable trust is one which divides legal ownership over the property from the *objects* for which that property may be used. This is the reason why we describe the reasons for which a charity exists as charitable objects or purposes.

To this day, a registered charity can be set up as a charitable trust. Typically, this involves a trust deed (i.e. document) which explicitly describes the operation of the trust from a governance perspective and which also includes the charitable objects and the dissolution clause. The operation of a trust is somewhat more formal than that for an unincorporated association as there are standard ways in which a trust operates and they are subject to the terms of the deed. But, they retain much of the flexibility that is inherent with an unincorporated association.

Again, similar to the unincorporated associations, the liabilities of the trust become the liabilities of the trustees of the trust automatically. It is for this reason that there is often little practical reason to prefer a trust over an unincorporated association. Nevertheless, a trust may be useful where the statute to which a corporation (see below) would be subject contains undesirable elements (such as requiring an audit). If an organization wanted to avoid organizing as a corporation subject to those rules and at the same time retain some level of formality in its operations, it may opt to organize as a trust.

Organizing as a trust may be a consideration in the same circumstances where one may consider using an unincorporated association — namely where the entity will exist solely to disburse funds rather than carry out charitable operations. Because a private foundation can be organized as a charitable trust but not an unincorporated association, families may consider setting up a trust for the dispersal of funds. In all other respects, a charitable trust that wishes to qualify for registration as a charity must comply with the same income tax rules that apply to every other registered charity. And, if circumstances arise, trustees may find themselves personally liable for the tax obligations for unremitted source deductions or even the revocation tax. A sample trust deed can be found on the website for this book at **www.runningacharity.ca**.

CORPORATIONS

The use of a corporation to organize as a charity is by far the most popular option. One reason may be that many people are familiar with corporations in a private company context involving shares, directors and officers. Corporations that operate charities (typically called charitable corporations) are, in fact, corporations without share capital. This means that instead of shareholders there are members. The members elect the directors and depending on the bylaws, the officers of the corporation may be elected by the members or appointed by the directors. There are no dividends if the corporation is registered as a charity.

Typically, the members of the corporation are admitted by the directors and the directors are elected by the members. The way out of this "chicken and egg" problem is that in some jurisdictions the original incorporators are directors who then admit members and in other jurisdictions they are members who then elect the directors. In yet others there are a group of incorporators and a separate group of directors.

Corporations are useful because of their strength in the areas in which the two previous forms of organization fail. First, they are a formally understood structure governed by a defined set of laws and bylaws. While these rules can become onerous on the organization, they do impart a measure of formality and tend to address almost all circumstances in which the corporation might find itself. So unlike the other organizations, there would rarely be a situation when the corporation is ungovernable for lack of direction.

Second, and perhaps more importantly, a corporation is a separate legal entity from its incorporators. For this reason, the liabilities of the organization are the liabilities of the corporation. For example, a debt owing to a supplier would be a debt of the corporation rather than a debt of the individual directors (assuming of course the contract was completed in the corporate name). Similarly, the revocation tax (see elsewhere in this book) would normally be a debt of the corporation rather than the debt of the directors. This is not to say that the directors can never become responsible for the debts of the corporation. In certain circumstances, the directors may be responsible for source deductions or the unpaid wages of employees or, in circumstances where directors behave negligently, they may become responsible for the debts of the corporation. (Note that this does not include debts related to improper use of gifts for which the donors have given specific instructions for their use).

JURISDICTION

Creating a corporation depends on the jurisdiction in which the organization plans to make its home base. Within Canada, an organization can be incorporated either federally or through any of the provinces and territories (some provinces have more than one law under which the corporation can be created). When the corporation is created it becomes subject to the regime described in that law under which it is incorporated. While every province has some law dealing with the creation of corporations without shares, the laws in this country are not standardized and so the responsibilities under various laws differ.

It is beyond the scope of this book to detail all the different laws and circumstances in which the corporation may find itself, but it is important to understand that in every province one at least has a choice; one may incorporate either federally or provincially. Nevertheless, a basic outline of the divergences from some of the more important elements of the *Canada Not-for-profit Corporations Act* follows.

CANADA NOT-FOR-PROFIT CORPORATIONS ACT

How many people are required to incorporate?	At least one, but soliciting corporations must have a minimum of three directors.
Are the first incorporators members or directors?	The incorporators do not assume either a member or director role by serving as incorporator.
Are there audit requirements? If so, at what level?	Soliciting corporations with less than $50,000 in revenue may have a *unanimous* vote not to have an audit, but they may audit.
	Soliciting corporations between $50,000 and $250,000 must have a financial review or an audit.
	Soliciting corporations with greater than $250,000 must have an audit.
What are the costs of incorporating?	Through Industry Canada's online registry system, $200. Otherwise, $250.
What are the costs of filing the annual return?	Through Industry Canada's online registry, $20. Otherwise, $40.
Additional Notes	The CNCA distinguishes between soliciting and non-soliciting corporations.
	Soliciting Corporation—Any CNCA corporation that has received in the previous fiscal year greater than $10,000 worth of donations or gifts requested from:
	• any person who is not a member, director, officer or employee of the corporation at the time of the request (or the spouse or family member of such a person);
	• grants or similar financial assistance received from the federal government or a provincial or municipal government, or an agency of such a government; or,
	• donations or gifts of money or other property from a soliciting corporation another corporation or entity that has received income in the manner described above.
	In addition to lower thresholds for audit requirements, Industry Canada publishes the financial statements of soliciting corporations.
	Ex officio directors are not permitted.

ALBERTA COMPANIES ACT

How many people are required to incorporate?	At least three.
Are the first incorporators members or directors?	Members.
Are there audit requirements? If so, at what level?	Audits are generally required for organizations with over $1,000,000 in revenue and with more than five members. Otherwise, in certain circumstances audits can be avoided.
What are the costs of incorporating?	$75.
What are the costs of filing the annual return?	No fee for filing.
Additional Notes	Both associations for charitable and for recreational purposes can be incorporated under the Companies Act, with the specific procedure being set out in Part 9 of the Act. If incorporated under Part 9, the association may have limited liability without including the phrase "limited" in its name).

ALBERTA SOCIETIES ACT

How many people are required to incorporate?	At least five over the age of 18.
Are the first incorporators members or directors?	Members.
Are there audit requirements? If so, at what level?	The by-laws of an Alberta society must contain provisions for the audit of accounts. Audited financial statements must be presented at a society's annual general meeting and signed by the society's auditor, setting out the society's income, disbursements, assets and liabilities and submitted to the government in the annual report.
What are the costs of incorporating?	$50.
What are the costs of filing the annual return?	No fee for filing.
Additional Notes	A corporation under the Alberta Societies Act may not have a purpose of carrying on a trade or business (s. 3).

BRITISH COLUMBIA SOCIETY ACT

How many people are required to incorporate?	At least one.
Are the first individuals members or directors?	Directors.
Are there audit requirements? If so, at what level?	May be avoided.
What are the costs of incorporating?	$130.
What are the costs of filing the annual return?	$40.
Additional Notes	The Society Act states that the incorporators may submit up to three proposed names using a name approval request form and a $30 fee. All filings, applications and maintenance are done online through the B.C. OnLine Portal.

MANITOBA CORPORATIONS ACT

How many people are required to incorporate?	At least one.
Are the first individuals members or directors?	Directors.
Are there audit requirements? If so, at what level?	No requirement, at company discretion. An audit can be dispensed with by unanimous consent of the members.
What are the costs of incorporating?	$165 (incorporation filing fee of $120 plus name reservation report $45.00).
What are the costs of filing the annual return?	$40.
Additional Notes	While the word "Manitoba" may not be used as the first word in a corporation with share capital, it can be in a corporation without share capital. The words "Association" or "Society" may also be used only by corporations without share capital.

NEW BRUNSWICK COMPANIES ACT

How many people are required to incorporate?	At least three.
Are the first incorporators members or directors?	Members.
Are there audit requirements? If so, at what level?	No requirements.
What are the costs of incorporating?	Between $62 and $212 depending on the assets of the proposed corporation.
What are the costs of filing the annual return?	$2.
Additional Notes	Section 18(2) prohibits a company which falls under its jurisdiction from any business or trade for the profit of its members.

NEWFOUNDLAND CORPORATIONS ACT

How many people are required to incorporate?	At least one.
Are the first incorporators members or directors?	Both.
Are there audit requirements? If so, at what level?	An audit can be dispensed with by unanimous consent of the members.
What are the costs of incorporating?	$70 if filed in paper form, $63 if filed electronically.
What are the costs of filing the annual return?	None.

NOVA SCOTIA SOCIETIES ACT

How many people are required to incorporate?	At least five.
Are the first incorporators members or directors?	Directors.
Are there audit requirements? If so, at what level?	Must file a financial statement with the Registrar (s.19) signed by an auditor, if there is one, or two directors otherwise.
What are the costs of incorporating?	$43.30.
What are the costs of filing the annual return?	$31.15.

NUNAVUT SOCIETIES ACT

How many people are required to incorporate?	At least five.
Are the first incorporator's members or directors?	Members.
Are there audit requirements? If so, at what level?	At the discretion of the by-laws — the act itself does not require an audit.
What are the costs of incorporating?	$50.
What are the costs of filing the annual return?	None.
Additional Notes	Annual Returns must include Financial Statements.

ONTARIO NOT-FOR-PROFIT CORPORATIONS ACT

How many people are required to incorporate?	At least one.
Are the first individuals members or directors?	Directors.
Are there audit requirements? If so, at what level?	• If a public benefit corporation, can pass extraordinary resolution to have a review engagement instead of an audit if gross revenue is less than $500,000; (if less than $100,000, can dispense with the review engagement in the same manner). • If not a public benefit corporation, can pass extraordinary resolution to have a review engagement instead of an audit if the corporation has more than $500,000 in annual revenue (if less than $500,000, can dispense in the same manner with any audit or review engagement).
What are the costs of incorporating?	$305.
What are the costs of filing the annual return?	None.
Additional Notes	The Act, when it comes into force, will replace the Corporations Act. Corporations without share capital who previously were under the Corporations Act will have three years to migrate to the new Act. After three years, they will be deemed to be subject to the new legislation. This act is similar to the Canada Not for Profit Corporations Act in many ways.

PEI COMPANIES ACT

How many people are required to incorporate?	At least three.
Are the first incorporators members or directors?	Members. However, at least three of the applicants for the letters patent must become the first directors.
Are there audit requirements? If so, at what level?	Open to specification in the by-laws.
What are the costs of incorporating?	$305 – ($265 incorporation fee and $40 mandatory name search performed by the PEI Consumer, Corporate and Insurance Services Division.)
What are the costs of filing the annual return?	$20 for corporations without share capital. $30 for corporations with share capital or cooperative.

QUEBEC COMPANIES ACT

How many people are required to incorporate?	At least three.
Are the first incorporators members or directors?	Members.
Are there audit requirements? If so, at what level?	None.
What are the costs of incorporating?	$205 – $225.50 ($150 application fee + $20 Name Search, within 60 days file your initial declaration; $35 for regular, or $52.50 for priority).
What are the costs of filing the annual return?	$35.
Additional Notes	Need to search for name of corporation (subject to Quebec language charter and limitations in code), pay fees for the search, and provide a copy of the search at time of registration. Primary name of the corporation must be in French.

SASKATCHEWAN NON-PROFIT CORPORATIONS ACT

How many people are required to incorporate?	At least one.
Are the first incorporators members or directors?	The act requires one incorporator and a separate list of first directors.
Are there audit requirements? If so, at what level?	If charitable corporation, may have a review engagement instead of an audit requirement if revenue is less than $250,000.
	If revenues are between $25,000 and $250,000 in the previous fiscal year, the requirement for an audit may be waived, but a "review" is required.
	If less than $25,000, can dispense in the same manner with the review engagement, voting on the resolution.
What are the costs of incorporating?	$85 ($50 incorporation fee, $15 mandatory newspaper notice, $20 mandatory name availability search).
What are the costs of filing the annual return?	$15 ($30 for late filing fee).
Additional Notes	Unless otherwise provided, the directors may make, amend or repeal bylaws. These stay in effect until the next general meeting and must be approved by the members then.

NORTHWEST TERRITORIES SOCIETIES ACT

How many people are required to incorporate?	At least five.
Are the first incorporators members or directors?	Members.
Are there audit requirements? If so, at what level?	Open to specification in the by-laws.
What are the costs of incorporating?	$50.
What are the costs of filing the annual return?	None.

YUKON SOCIETIES ACT	
How many people are required to incorporate?	At least five.
Are the first incorporators members or directors?	There is a separate list of first directors.
Are there audit requirements? If so, at what level?	No specifications for audit in the Act.
What are the costs of incorporating?	$30.
What are the costs of filing the annual return?	$10.

Incorporating

While there are different laws in every jurisdiction, the process for incorporating is practically the same in each. In order to incorporate, a group is generally required of three to five incorporators, who will serve as the originators of the corporation. As stated earlier, in some provinces these incorporators are the first directors, and in others they are the first members.

An organization will also require charitable objects as described elsewhere in this book, and, at the CRA's insistence, it should also contain a dissolution clause. This clause will require that upon dissolution as a corporation the assets of the corporation will be transferred to other qualified donees. It bears mentioning that an organization will probably lose its charitable status before dissolution. In such a circumstance, by operation of the revocation tax the organization will already have distributed all of its assets, and as a result the organization will have no assets left for distribution when it is dissolved. Alternatively, it may have distributed all of its assets at the time of deregistration but then built up additional assets *after* deregistration. If that is the case, then the organization may wish to revisit the dissolution clause after its revocation as a charity in order that it may distribute its assets in a different manner. Organizations that are contemplating a dissolution clause may also seek to limit the clause in order that assets be distributed out to organizations with similar charitable objects.

Unfortunately, it is impossible here to conduct a thorough review of each of the various laws in the different provinces which may apply to organizations seeking incorporation. However, organizations may wish to approach the decision with some forethought as certain laws have certain requirements which they may find undesirable. For example, certain laws require audits at different financial thresholds. Given that audits are expensive, an organization might wish to seek a higher threshold at which it must seek the audit. Some laws are less vigorous in their governance requirements, while others may make amalgamation or continuance into another law difficult or impossible. For this reason, qualified counsel should be sought out that can help advise a prospective corporation about the different regimes which may be available to the organization.

Maintenance

Corporations are designed to be "living" entities, which means that they require maintenance in order that their operations and decisions are legally valid. Most of the obligations are apparent from a thorough reading of the bylaws and statute. For example, organizations require a meeting of the members which allows the members to elect the directors. Another provision may indicate that directors have term limits and so should not be occupying their position any longer than is allowed.

In another vein, organizations have legal requirements imposed upon them by statute. For example, there may be a corporate information return to be filed every year, including the names of all the directors and their addresses. For example, the *Canada Not-for-profit Corporations Act* requires that each director of the corporation be known to the government and that the government be informed within fifteen days of a move of the residential address of any of the directors.

The actual maintenance requirements of each corporation depends on the law under which it was incorporated, but it can be assumed that:

- each entity is required to have a meeting
- the members must be admitted properly to the corporation
- the directors must be properly elected
- there must be an annual meeting of the members allowing the members to review the financial statements, elect the directors and appoint the auditors if required

It is important that the bylaws be read and consulted each time there is a meeting or any time there is doubt about how the corporation should operate. Often we have seen people simply assume that bylaws were "suggestions" or that they could be safely ignored. This is not the case. Bylaws have been developed over time by people with experience in the operations of corporations, they are meant to be followed *in all circumstances*. The trouble with ignoring the bylaws for the sake of expediency is that eventually the corporation runs into a situation where the legal validity of a decision of the corporation may be questioned. If the bylaws had been followed properly up to that time, then there can be no doubt that the decisions of the corporation taken are legally valid. However, there are circumstances where a step missed forty years previous can affect the legal validity of a decision today. For this reason, we recommend that bylaws and statutes be consulted consistently to ensure that decisions are properly made.

Dissolution

Eventually the time may come when the corporation is to be dissolved. Generally, the process by which the dissolution may take place is outlined within the organizing statute. However, dissolution of corporations must be made in consultation with the relevant legal regime (this is generally the law under which the corporation was originally incorporated).

Assuming that an organization has already met its charity law obligations after revocation, the revocation tax rules would likely operate to make the corporation an empty shell; and in these circumstances the dissolution process is fairly simple. Typically it involves the filing of dissolution documents with the relevant government ministry and certain public notices. This in itself necessitates that the organization has filed all the necessary tax documents and owes no money to the government or anyone else. In these circumstances the corporation can be dissolved.

If the corporation is not dissolved and simply exists as a moribund entity, the liabilities of the directors may continue. Generally, potential liabilities of the corporation and its directors will cease after a certain time period. The time period often starts to run when the directors cease to act as such. For some directors, (usually those left unable to find their own replacements — like a corporate version of musical chairs, the ones left standing when the music stops) this may require dissolution of the corporation in order that the timeline can begin. Therefore, directors may want to ensure that the corporation is properly dissolved as early as possible.

In certain circumstances, usually involuntary to the directors, the corporation may be dissolved at the behest of the government. Generally, this happens when the corporation fails to file proper documentation with the relevant government ministry. In these circumstances the corporation may be informed by that office that it no longer exists as a corporation. When this happens, and if the organization is a registered charity, it will become liable for the revocation tax. Although, in practice, the CRA (and sometimes the charity) is often unaware of the dissolution. Thus, missing a filing may result not only in loss of corporate status it may also result in the loss of charitable status and the loss of all the assets of the corporation.

Amalgamation

At times, corporations may seek out others with a similar mandate to gain efficiencies by amalgamating the two entities. Amalgamations of such corporations can be somewhat difficult because the laws that govern them can be outdated and contain insufficient legal means to effect an amalgamation. Of course, this assumes that both corporations are governed by the same law. Where the corporations exist under different laws it may be necessary to continue one of them into the others act (if possible) so that an amalgamation is possible.

In the world of registered charities, amalgamations are rare. The transfer of assets between registered charities can be effected rather simply, and since the membership of such entities can expand without much difficulty, "mergers" are generally conducted as transfers of assets from one entity to another and subscription of new members from the abandoned corporation to the new corporation. In either case, the amalgamation should not be attempted without the benefit of advice from counsel experienced in this area.

OPERATING EXTRA-PROVINCIALLY

Many entities operate in more than one province. It would be too easy to assume that they could do so without complying with some additional laws. In fact, each province will assert some new law which may make operations in that province more complicated. For example, operating in Alberta or Saskatchewan may require registration under one of the fundraising acts, and operation in Ontario requires certain compliance with the office of the Ontario Public Guardian and Trustee. To make matters worse, creating a base of operations in any of the operations may require specific filings. Thus, an organization may be subjected to filings in each of the various provinces simply because it has a base of operations as defined by that province's legislation.

In the charts below, it is only corporations which must file the documentation relating to extra-provincial corporations. The rules for fundraising and charitable registration at the office of the Public Guardian and Trustee apply to all entities operating in Ontario regardless of whether or not they are incorporated.

British Columbia

Extra-provincial registration

Steps to extra-provincial registration

1. Submit a name request — a name request reservation number will be assigned once a name has been approved and reserved. This step can be completed at this website https://www.bcregistry.ca/societies/.

2. Use the name request reservation number to complete the rest of the registration application. A BC-based representative will be necessary. This step can be completed at this website https://www.bcregistry.ca/societies/.

The filing fee online is $30.00. A name will be reserved for 56 calendar days, and any renewals of the name reservation will require the payment of the reservation fee.

Maintaining an extra-provincial society

To maintain an extra-provincial registration, the society must file online:

- A verified copy of amendments to the constitution and by-laws within a month of any taking place. Each change requires a $50.00 filing fee.

- Any changes to the address of the head office, directors or the addresses, name or attorney for service. Each filing requires a $15.00 filing fee.

- The Annual Report, filed within thirty days of each general meeting; a $40.00 fee applies.

These forms may be populated and submitted online at: http://www.gov.bc.ca/societiesonline.

Alberta

Application documents

The Corporation should apply to the Registrar by submitting certified copies, in English, of the following documents:

- a Statement of Registration

- the charter (letter of incorporation, and any supplementary letters patent)

- the name or operating name and the NUANS Alberta Search Report

- the appointment of an attorney for service and if applicable, the alternative attorney for service; their name and address

Once the application is complete, applicants should submit it to an authorized service provider who will examine the application and confer upon the organization a Certificate of Registration. Authorized service providers are private sector firms that have levels of accreditation for the various services they provide. Service fees are not regulated by the government and so there may be price differentials between authorized service providers. The service fee to register an extra-provincial corporation in Alberta is $275. However, a non-profit corporation can apply for a reduction by sending a letter on the organization's letterhead to the Registrar seeking an exemption by stating that they are a non-profit entity. The fee with the exemption is $75 and the exemption is submitted by an authorized service provider.

Name

The corporation's name must conform to the requirements of a corporate name under the ABCA regulations. The name also:

- must not be prohibited;

- must not be identical or similar (confusing or misleading) to another corporation incorporated in Alberta or federally, or another extra-provincial corporation continued in Alberta.

The Registrar may approve of the use of an operating name should there be a conflict, and this operating name may be cancelled at any time. Under the operating name the corporation may incur the rights, debts and liabilities as if it were registered under its real name. The corporation may be sued under its own name, its operating name, or both.

Attorney

Every extra-provincial corporation must appoint for itself an attorney for service to represent the corporation in Alberta. The attorney need not be a lawyer. Upon death or resignation of an appointed attorney, the extra-provincial corporation must appoint another and register the appointment.

Maintaining the registration

Amendments

A registered corporation must send to the Register through an authorized service provider:

- certified copies of all amendments filed in the home jurisdiction within one month of their taking effect

- notices of change if the attorney, directors, office address, or directors' addresses change

Annual returns

The corporation must render annual returns to the Registrar no later than the last day of the anniversary month of its incorporation in the other jurisdiction. The form is available online. The filing fee for the Annual Return is $50, and the filing is done through an authorized service provider.

No act of the extra-provincial corporation will be invalid only by reason of the corporation not being registered or the act being contrary or unauthorized by the charter of the corporation or laws of the incorporating jurisdiction.

Fundraising

Charitable fundraising, conducted by professional fundraisers and charities themselves, is regulated by the *Charitable Fund-raising Act*. Charities, whether incorporated or not, must register if they make solicitations for contributions and if:

- they use a fundraising business to solicit contributions;

- they intend to raise more than $25,000 in gross contributions in its financial year from solicitations of individuals in Alberta; or

- they raised more than $25,000 in gross contributions in its financial year, in which case they must register within 45 days of receiving $25,000 in gross contributions.

Depending on the organizational and operational structure of the extra-provincial charity, it may be exempt from the above restrictions. For example, no registration is required by an unincorporated charity group that is affiliated with another organization and the affiliate controls the distributions of the contributions the charity receives during the financial year.

Only charities registered under the ACFA can employ a fundraising business to solicit contributions on its behalf.

A charity *must* register if their solicitations are:

- direct or indirect requests for contribution where it is stated or implied that it will be used by a charitable organization or purpose (keeping in mind the broad definition of such under the ACFA); or

- requests for contribution through a direct or indirect request to buy goods or services through which it is stated or implied that some or the entire purchase price will be used by a charitable organization or purpose.

A charity *does not need* to register if their solicitations only are:

- made by a member of a charity to their family members;

- for goods or services used by the charity for a non-charitable (ex: administrative) purposes; or

- through a licensed gaming activity such as raffles, bingos or casinos.

Steps to register a charity for fundraising purposes:

1. Fill out the Application for Charitable Organization and fee ($60.00).

2. If registering for the first time, submit copies of solicitation materials and telemarketing scripts that will be used for fundraising.

Registration is for one year. Further information is available through Service Alberta online.

Donors' rights

If a charity conducts solicitations with intent to gross more than $25,000 in a financial year, it is required to provide, upon request by donors, copies of recently audited financial statements, the portion of gross contributions received that were used directly for the charitable purposes of the charity, reasonable detail about where and how the contributions it solicits will be spent and other information required by the regulations. All contributions made in the course of solicitations must be receipted if requested, except for the direct or indirect requests to buy goods.

Receipting and record-keeping

Charities must keep complete financial records for fundraising activities going back at least three years.

These include:

- original financial statements
- records of all solicitations;
- records of the bank account (if any) used for deposits and any payments from that account
- names of the signing officers for the bank account
- samples of the information given to potential donors, including publications and phone scripts
- copies of the fundraising agreement and any amendments
- copies of cash receipts

Saskatchewan

The application should include:

- the fee ($65 ($50 fee + mandatory Gazette publishing fee of $15))
- copy of the articles of incorporation
- a power of attorney

The Director will also require a Request for Name Availability Search and Reservation, which has a $20 fee.

Power of attorney

The corporation is required to name and register an individual residing in Saskatchewan in a power of attorney unless the corporation has a director or officer resident in Saskatchewan.

Name

A corporation should apply to reserve its name or alternate name through the "Request for Name Availability Search and Reservation Form." Any alternative trade name must be registered under the *Business Names Registration Act.*

Changes

The corporation must notify the Director within fifteen days of any changes in address of head office, attorney, or directors. Copies of any articles of amendment must also be sent to the Director.

Annual return

The corporation must file an annual return with the Director.

Fundraising

Charities should be aware of the rules regarding solicitations for contributions whether by telephone, door-to-door or another form. The latter may include operating a web site that solicits, or receives contributions from Saskatchewan residents. Telephone and door-to-door solicitations are allowed between 8:00 am and 9:00 pm. Contributions may be for money, services or goods, or any pledge or promise for contributions.

If a charity hires a fundraising business to solicit on its behalf, the business must be licensed under the *Charitable Fund-raising Businesses Act* (the "CFBA"). The fundraising agreement must be in writing and in the manner and form prescribed in the Act which requires that the Agreement:

a) must be in writing;

b) must include:

    i) all the terms and conditions between the parties respecting the fund-raising, including:

        A) the duties and responsibilities of both parties; and

        B) the manner in which the fund-raising agreement may be terminated;

    ii) an estimate of the amount of contributions to be received and an estimate of the expenses and costs of the fund-raising;

    iii) if the solicitations will involve selling goods or services, a description of the goods or services and the specific price for which the goods or services will be sold;

    iv) the address of:

        A) the charitable organization; and

        B) the licensee;

    v) the name and telephone number of the contact person for:

        A) the charitable organization; and

        B) the licensee; and

    vi) *any other prescribed matter; and*

   c)   must set out:

      i)   the solicitation method or methods to be used;

      ii)   the remuneration of the licensee, being either or a combination of the following:

         A)   a specified amount of money;

         B)   a specified percentage of gross contributions; and

      iii)   the method by which the remuneration is to be paid.

   d)   Every licensee that enters into a fundraising agreement pursuant to subsection (1) shall provide a copy of that agreement to the registrar within the prescribed period prior to commencing a campaign of solicitation.

A soliciting charity must provide, to any person of whom they are requesting a contribution, among other things:

- the remuneration being paid to the third party fundraiser
- various contact information of the organization on whose behalf the donations are being solicited
- the charitable purpose for which the donations are being used
- the jurisdiction in which the funds will be spent

They must also provide to anyone who requests it:

- copies of recent financial statements
- the portion of gross revenues that were used on charitable purposes in the last year
- an estimate of the amount that will be used on charitable purposes in the current year
- information about where and how the revenues are spent, and information regarding any fundraising businesses used

Manitoba

Extra-provincial registration

Philanthropic non-share capital corporations (i.e. charities) must register under the *Corporations Act* of Manitoba in order to conduct business in Manitoba. Registration with the Companies Office accords the entity with legal personality. Registration is valid for three years and may be renewed by the registrant; otherwise, the business name will be cancelled. The Application for Registration fee is $120.

All the necessary forms for registration, renewal and changes are available online and can now be processed online as well.

Name

Charities may reserve a name online at a fee of $45 and payment is by credit card only.

- The name should consist of a distinctive element, a descriptive element, and end with a legal element (for corporate name only).
- The name should not be confusingly similar to an existing name or trademark.
- The name must not be objectionable.

The charity must provide the reason for the reservation, the name, the nature of the business and the location of the business and all other relevant information. For extra-provincial and federal registrations, if the name is in both French and English there is only need for one registration.

With every document submitted, whether to register, renew or change, a "Request for Service Form" must be submitted as well.

Maintaining registration

Changes

- Change of business name ($45 fee applies)
- Change of address (no fee), and
- Change of directors (no fee) declaration must be given to the Companies Office as applicable.

Annual return

An extra-provincial or federally registered charity must file annual returns in Manitoba, at a cost of $40.00 for non-share capital corporations. It should be filed as of the last day of the anniversary month every year.

Registration of unincorporated associations

An unincorporated association may submit a "Request for Name Notation" in order to establish a presence in the Companies Office records for three years and can be changed or renewed or dissolved thereafter. The unincorporated association still must reserve and register its business name.

Ontario

Extra-provincial registration

Registration is completed by filing an *Initial Return/Notice of Change* (Form 2) with the Central Production and Verification Services Branch at 393 University Ave, Suite 200, Toronto, Ontario M5G 2M2 within sixty days of carrying on the activities in Ontario. Non-share capital corporations must include in the Initial Return:

- the name of the corporation
- the Ontario corporation number
- the date of the incorporation/amalgamation, whichever is more recent
- the name of the jurisdiction of incorporation/amalgamation referred to above
- address of the corporation's head or registered office
- the date the corporation commenced activities in Ontario and/or ceased (if any)
- name and office address of the chief officer or manager in Ontario, if any and the date they assumed the role, and/or when it ceased
- address of the principal office in Ontario
- if the corporation is required to have an agent for service in Ontario, the contact information for the agent and the Ontario corporation number if the agent is a corporation
- preferred language of communication
- the immediate former name of the corporation

And if any information on the initial return changes, an extra-provincial corporation must file the *Initial Return/Notice of Change* (Form 2). A copy of the form is available at **www.runningacharity.ca**.

An extra-provincial corporation can use any name other than its corporate name, unless that name in Ontario is prohibited by the regulations, is the same or similar to an existing organization or individual in Ontario, or would be likely to deceive the public. To ensure that there is no confusion with existing names, corporations should conduct an "Enhanced Business Name Search." It is recommended that the corporation contact a search house to conduct an Ontario NUANS name search report.

Acquiring property in Ontario

Within one month of acquisition, corporations that are charities must report to the Office of the Public Guardian and Trustee (PGT) certain donations given to it, such as real or personal property, or interests therein, or the proceeds vested in an executor or trustee for a charitable purpose trust. Although there is a set form for this report, the notice to the PGT should include:

- a statement of the nature of the property
- a copy of the instrument of conveyance
- detailed information about the corporation

Quebec

Extra-provincial registration

Registrants must file a Declaration of Registration. This is done via an online form. Paper forms can be attained by contacting Services Quebec at 1.800.361.9596.

Fee for not-for-profit corporations if filed within 60 days of beginning operations in Quebec:

- Regular: $35.00
- Priority: $52.50

As part of the process, the registrant must submit a "Name Research Report Application" and "Name Reservation Application."

The corporate name:

- must conform to the Charter of the French languages
- must be reserved
- cannot be prohibited
- cannot be misleading

In addition, the corporation must declare a French version of the name used in Quebec and use the name in association with the activities unless it is only a surname and given name.

Maintaining the registration

Registrants must file an Annual Declaration every year. This is done via an online form. Paper forms can be attained by contacting Services Quebec at 1.800.361.9596.

The Annual Declaration should be filed between May 15 and November 15.

Fee for not-for-profit corporations if filed on time:

- Regular: no fee
- Priority: $17

Fee if filed late:

- Regular: $17
- Priority: $34

Registrants must also notify the enterprises registrar of any amendments during the year. Amending Declarations are at no cost unless a registrant opts for priority processing, in which case a $17.00 fee applies.

New Brunswick

Extra-provincial registration

Where an extra-provincial corporation carries on business in New Brunswick without a purpose of profit, the Director at Service New Brunswick may exempt the corporation from corporate registration requirements under the Business Corporations Act. If an extra-provincial corporation chooses to register, it must do so within thirty days of carrying on business in New Brunswick (NB). Registration gives the corporation the power to commence or maintain any proceedings or actions in a NB court. A proceeding may be maintained if the corporation becomes registered during the proceedings.

If the corporation chooses to apply for the exemption, it should submit the following:

1. A letter indicating that the corporation does not carry on business for the purpose of gain and that it wishes to apply for an exemption.
2. A copy of incorporation documents and any amendments.
3. Form 25, Appointment of Attorney for Service, naming a resident of New Brunswick as its agent.
4. Form 25.1, Consent to Act as Attorney for Service.
5. Fee of $100 payable to Service New Brunswick.

If the corporation instead chooses to register, it must submit:

1. Form 26, Statement of Registration Extra-Provincial Corporation (in duplicate).
2. Form 24, Appointment of Attorney for Service (in duplicate).
3. Form 25.1, Consent to Act as Attorney for Service (in duplicate).
4. The "Additional Information Form."

5. A copy of the incorporation documents.

6. A New Brunswick NUANS name reservation report generated in the last 90 days.

7. Fee of $212.00 (or $312.00 for expedited service) payable to Service New Brunswick.

Name

An extra-provincial corporation cannot be registered under a name that is:

- deceptively similar to an existing business name without license
- prohibited
- reserved for another business

If it must change its name, the extra-provincial corporation may submit the form "Certificate of Business Name or Renewal of Business Name" and the "Additional Information Form" pursuant to the *Partnerships and Business Names Registration Act*. Applicants should conduct a NUANS name search report no more than 90 days prior to filing for a name. A Certificate of Business Name costs $112.00 and the Renewal of Business Name costs $62.00.

The government should be notified of any change of name through Form 32.1 "Notice of Change of Name" to the Director to reserve a name for an extra-provincial corporation for ninety days.

Maintaining the registration

Attorney for service

The attorney must notify the corporation and Director within sixty days if he or she intends to resign. The new appointment must be sent to the Director. A $50.00 fee applies to appoint or change an attorney for service.

Changes

The registered extra-provincial corporation must notify the Director of any change in its name and the resulting amendment of its constituting documents. A $112.00 fee applies to change the name, or $212.00 for expedited service. As well, within one month of any changes, the Director must be notified of any changes in the address in New Brunswick and the membership of the charity's board of directors or governing body. This can be filed at www.snb.ca.

Annual returns

The registered extra-provincial corporation must file annual returns with the Director.

The charity should use the appropriate form or may also file with it its annual return from the incorporating jurisdiction. The charity may elect to make its anniversary month the same as its incorporating month. A $25.00 fee applies to select an anniversary month. To file online an annual fee of $200.00 applies or $220.00 for a paper filing by mail.

Nova Scotia

Extra-provincial registration

There is no legislation specifically requiring an extra-provincial charity to register as an entity in Nova Scotia in order to acquire legal status. In conversation with Representatives of the Registry of Joint Stock Companies, it was advised that an extra-provincial charity incorporate in Nova Scotia if it wants to acquire property, open a bank account or obtain insurance etc. Information about incorporating as a society is available online or by contacting the Registry of Joint Stock Companies at 1.800.225.8227.

Prince Edward Island

Name

Extra-provincial corporations may request a business name by contacting the Consumer, Corporate and Insurance Services Division. The cost of the NUANS name search and registration for three years is $105 payable to the Provincial Treasurer of PEI. The cost of renewal is $50 for each subsequent three-year period.

Steps to registration

1. Request a NUANS name search to reserve a business name.

2. Submit the "Application for Registration" and the fee of $275.

This can be mailed to:
The Office of the Attorney General, Consumer, Corporate and Insurance Services
PO Box 2000,
Charlottetown, PEI
CIA 7N8

It can also be submitted in person to:
95 Rochford Street, 4th floor
Charlottetown, PEI
C1A 3T6

Maintaining the registration

Registrants may renew their certificate of registration within six months of the expiration of the most recent certificate by filing a notice of renewal of registration to the Director.

Notify the Director of any changes within 30 days of a change in name, or amalgamation.

Newfoundland and Labrador

Unlike other provinces which allow a certain period between commencing operations and registration, in Newfoundland and Labrador (NL) the registration must take place *before* operations can be commenced in the province.

In order to register a corporation must:

- File Statement for Registration — Extra-Provincial Company Form 24.
- File a Power of Attorney Form 26.
- File a Statutory Declaration Form 25, attesting to truth of registration and include in the application two certified copies of the statute, certificate or other constituting document of the corporation.
- Pay a fee of $260.

Maintaining the registration

To maintain the registration the corporation must:

- file the Annual Return — Extra-Provincial Company Form 28 with the $200 fee (or $180 if filing online);
- notify the Commercial Registrations Division of any changes in head office by filing the Notice of Change of Chief Place of Business Form 32;
- notify of any change in the registered office in NL by filing the Notice of Change of Registered Office in Newfoundland and Labrador;
- notify of any changes in the power of attorney should the attorney change;
- within one month, notify of any changes in the name of the registrant, in the constituting documents or in the objects of the company.

Name

The name of the extra-provincial corporation must be displayed or affixed outside the head office in NL. There is no independent business name registration in Newfoundland.

Yukon

Steps to registering

Within thirty days of carrying on business in the Yukon the corporation must:

- appoint an attorney for service;
- notify the registrar of the address of the head office in the incorporating jurisdiction;
- file a Statement of Registration with the $300 fee; and
- reserve a business name or assumed name if the business name is prohibited.

The NUANS name search costs $40.00 and the reservation of an assumed name costs $75.00.

Name

The name should be distinctive, i.e. not the same or similar to a business name already registered with Corporate Affairs in the Yukon. It should also indicate a legal element. Once registered, applicants should file the "Declaration of Business Name Form."

Maintaining the registration

In order to maintain the registration:

- the corporation must keep up-to-date records by notifying the registrar of any changes, amendments have a fee of $100 using the Notice of Change of Statement for Registration as an Extra-Territorial Corporation;
- if there are any changes to the Directors or the Directors' address, there is no fee;
- if there are any changes to the Appointment of Attorney for Service and Alternative Attorney of Extra-Territorial Corporation, there is no fee; and
- the corporation must file an Annual Return for a fee of ($100) on or before the last day of the anniversary month (the month in which the corporation became subject to the YBCA).

Northwest Territories

Steps to registering

In order to register a corporation must:

- conduct a name search and reserve request if the corporation is not federally incorporated for a $25.00 fee;

- send to the Registrar a certified copy of the constituting documents of the corporation and any amendments;

- provide a certificate no more than thirty days old of the good standing of the corporation in the incorporating jurisdiction;

- register the address of the corporation by filing, in duplicate, Form 21 "Notice of Registered Office" or "Notice of Change of Registered Office Extra-Territorial Corporation";

- submit Form 18 "Statement of Registration Extra-Territorial Corporation;" and,

- pay the filing fee of $100.

The Department of Justice, Corporate Registry has informational booklets on filling out the required forms available online.

Registration of extra-territorial corporate name

Except for a federally-incorporated corporation, there are restrictions on the name of the business. It must not contain prohibited words as per the NWTBCA Regulations, is not the same or misleadingly similar to an existing registered corporation in the NWT, and is not a reserved name. If there is no problem with the name, the Registry will reserve the name for 90 days.

Maintaining the registration

Registered extra-provincial corporations should:

- maintain a registered office in the NWT at all times, that is accessible to the public during normal business hours;

- within thirty days, inform the government of any changes in the address, name, or constituting documents and provide certified copies; and

- file an annual return with the Registrar in the anniversary month of the incorporation or amalgamations.

Nunavut

Extra-territorial registration

Registration

In order to register a corporation must submit:

- a name search request, this is not applicable for numbered or federal companies, the fee for this is $25;

- a Form 18, Statement of Registration Extra-Territorial Corporation, and a Form 21, Notice of Registered Officer in duplicate;

- certified true copies of all charter documents, including amendments;

- a Certificate of Status of Good Standing no more than 30 days old from the corporation's home jurisdiction; and

- a $100 filing fee.

A complete guide containing all of the forms and submissions guide is located on the Corporate Registry website at http://nunavutlegalregistries.ca. Documents are submitted in PDF format via email; forms can be submitted by fax, mail or by hand, but it is preferred that submissions be done via email.

Registration of extra-territorial corporate name

Except for a federally incorporated corporation, there are restrictions on the name of the business. It must not contain prohibited words as per the Nunavut *Business Corporation Act*, is not the same or misleadingly similar to an existing registered corporation in the Nunavut, and is not a reserved name. If there is no problem with the name, the Registry will reserve the name for 90 days.

Maintaining the registration

Registered extra-provincial corporations should:

- maintain a registered office in the Nunavut at all times that is accessible to the public during normal business hours;

- within 30 days, inform the government of any changes in the address, name, or constituting documents and provide certified copies; and

- file an annual return with the Registrar in the anniversary month of the incorporation or amalgamations. The fee for this is $70.

As stated above, the following forms shall be submitted as described above, with the preference being via email.

3 | What is a Charity?

Most Canadians understand that a charity is an organization that undertakes good deeds for the benefit of others or some cause understood to be charitable. However, the legal meaning of charity differs from the understood lay meaning, and an organization seeking registered charity status with the CRA will not succeed without complying with the legal meaning. This chapter is intended to review the legal basis on which an organization can qualify to be a charity.

The law does not assume that every organization that undertakes a cause for the public benefit is necessarily a charity. Fundamentally, if an organization wants to qualify as a charity under Canadian law it has two choices: either it finds a case which found that the cause in question was charitable in law, or it falls under some legal mechanism which effectively gives the organization the same benefits as other registered charities.

Of course, it is beyond the scope of this book to detail every case that has been decided in this area over the past 400 years, so in this chapter we present a summarized version of the law. An organization interested in undertaking work in some novel area related to a cause already understood to be charitable should contact qualified legal counsel.

CHARITIES VS NOT-FOR-PROFIT VS FOR-PROFIT

A registered charity is defined in the *Income Tax Act* as one formed for charitable purposes, but there is no statutory definition of "charitable purposes." As discussed in the introduction, a charitable purpose is one where a court has found that the cause to be undertaken falls within what the law understands to be charitable. Moreover, charitable purposes do not guarantee registration as a charity with the CRA.

It is important to understand that a not-for-profit is different from a charity, and different rules apply to such an organization. A not-for-profit is one which is *not a charity at law* but, like a charity, will not provide any benefits (generally payments) to the members of the group. Political groups (although not parties) and recreational organizations are typically not-for-profits. While in common parlance a not-for-profit and a charity are considered interchangeable, they are *not* the same thing, and charities should be careful about referring to themselves as a not-for-profit as it implies that the group cannot issue charitable donation tax receipts.

A for-profit organization is one which is neither a not-for-profit nor a registered charity. Organizations should take care that they are not an unregistered charity, as such groups might find themselves falling within the definition of for-profit organizations for tax purposes. Such organizations are subject to tax on *all* of their income and of course cannot issue charitable donation tax receipts.

OTHER QUALIFIED DONEES

Canadians understand that donations to registered charities result in tax receipts which can be used to create donation tax credits on their income tax returns. However, registered charities are only one of several groups that can issue tax receipts. These organizations are called qualified donees. The list includes the following types of organizations:

a) Registered Charities

b) Registered Canadian Amateur Athletic Associations

c) The United Nations or an agency of the United Nations

d) Federal, Provincial or municipal governments, or a public body performing a function of government (generally refers to the government of an Indian reserve)

e) Certain not-for-profit housing corporations

f) Certain foreign universities

g) Certain other foreign organizations that have been granted this status

h) Registered National Arts Service Organizations

i) Registered Journalism Organizations

The actual list of universities worldwide is very long and includes many of the universities in the USA and most other universities which have at least some Canadian students. There is a process available for universities that wish to be included on this list. Such universities should contact qualified legal counsel if they seek to be included.

The list of organizations to which the government gives gifts to in a year has become more transparent in recent years but is fundamentally discretionary to the government. It is clear that the government has allowed itself the ability to include some foreign organizations for both political and practical purposes. It would be unlikely that any organization could simply "wish" to be included on this list and arrange for it to happen without some compelling reason for the government to involve itself in this arrangement.

CHARITABLE OBJECTS

The purposes for which a charity must be organized are known as charitable objects. They can be found in the organizing documents of every type of charitable entity. Typically, these statements serve to limit the organization's ability to engage in any activity other than what is included in the objects. Over the past 400 years the law in this area has been divided into four categories, or heads. A proposed object that does not fall within one of the four heads is not eligible for registration.

There are two fundamental elements to a charitable object. The first is that the object itself must be found to have been charitable at law in a previous case, or the object must otherwise be analogous to some previously decided case. The second element is that the manner in which the object is to be fulfilled must be for the public benefit. It is not sufficient that the cause to be undertaken is to benefit the public — it must meet the element of having been decided to be charitable in law.

Entities will only get registered as charities if their objects allow them to pursue charitable purposes and nothing but charitable purposes. The CRA will also refuse registration where it finds that the entity has an unstated collateral purpose as evidenced by the entity's activities. So, it is important that the objects be broad enough to encompass the organization's activities, but tightly worded to prevent the organization from pursuing activities which would not qualify as charitable. For this reason, most successful organizations have between one and four objects and no more.

The objects need not contain a list of every constituent activity necessary to accomplish the final objective. For example, objects never include things like buying vegetables when the overall purpose is to feed the hungry. Necessary components and ancillary activities to pursuing the object need not be mentioned. On the other hand, the CRA generally does require some limited in wording in the objects that define the activity to be undertaken in pursuit of the charitable activity; for example, to relieve poverty by teaching vocational skills — rather than simply 'to relieve poverty'. The CRA also generally prefers a clause stating the eligible beneficiary group, although from a technical perspective this is often unnecessary.

Properly-drafted charitable objects are critical to a successful application for registered charity status. It is not sufficient to rely on the fact that there are other organizations out there that do similar work, or to provide a listing of the things you intend the organization to do. Rather, a considered, researched approach should be employed to ensure that the charity has the right to do what it needs to do — and to give the CRA confidence that the organization is deserving of registration.

CHARITABLE HEADS

Advancement of education

Advancement of education is perhaps the most controversial of charitable heads.

Technically, advancing education in the charitable sense means formally training the mind, advancing the knowledge or abilities of the recipient, or improving the useable branch of human knowledge. This would involve running a school, conducting and publishing research, or providing academic scholarships to attend university.

Advancing education does not mean convincing others of a position. This argument has been rejected several times by the Courts in looking at issues of abortion. The law is clear on the point that there is no room to define education as being one where a charity ostensibly tries to "educate" others of its position.

Generally speaking, education should be understood in an almost antiseptic way. Typical educational programs that teach the basics of science, language, math and the social sciences qualify. This does not mean that taking a position on a side in an academic debate is prohibited; rather that both elements of the academic debate must be presented to the students.

Organizations that seek charitable status under this head will be asked by the CRA for confirmation of the curriculum, the qualifications of the teachers, the facilities, and the students who will receive the education. Such groups should typically provide the type of education that one would expect to find in most schools and universities on topics that are generally offered in these organizations. Continuing education programs for adults will also qualify as long as the education is not intended to further the recipients' professional earnings, and otherwise meets the restrictions placed on charities operating in this area.

Advancement of religion

Advancing religion in the charitable sense means manifesting, promoting, sustaining or increasing belief in a religion. To qualify as a religion there must be faith in a higher unseen power such as a god, supreme being or entity; worship or reverence; and a particular and comprehensive system of doctrines and observances.

The key element to the advancement of religion is the requirement that there be an element of theistic worship. Judaism, Christianity, Islam, and Hinduism all have organizations registered in Canada. Buddhism and Taoism can also be registered in Canada but they are exceptions to the rule requiring a theistic element. There are, however, some notable exceptions, including Scientology, Jainism and Shinto. While it may be offensive that in today's multicultural Canada there are some religious groups that do not qualify for registered charity status, there is little the CRA can do to change this. The only substantive change to this policy will come when the issue is litigated to the Federal Court of Appeal by an organization refused registration as a charity.

Nevertheless, given the sensitivity of the issue, officers of the Charities Directorate have been known to bend over backwards to find some other grounds upon which to register groups which do not meet the technical definition of the advancement of religion.

Typically, organizations that advance religion will be involved in missionary work or outreach, operation of a church, synagogue, mosque, or temple, with regular worship services, or the conduct of religious schools.

Relief of poverty

Relieving poverty means providing relief for the poor and not just the destitute. "Poor" is defined as anyone lacking essential amenities available to the general public. The test of amenities available to the general public does not necessarily mean that if an individual in a poor region lacks clean water (as does everyone else in that region), the provision of clean water is not charitable since no one in the area has it. Rather, it is understood that there are certain basic requirements of life that everyone needs, and providing these requirements is considered charitable. Examples include providing food and basic health care, tuition subsidies for low-income individuals, and micro-loan financing so that the poor can set up their own businesses.

Generally speaking, there is a presumption of public benefit for the relief of poverty. This means that the CRA will not generally question the public benefit nature of the relief of poverty. Nevertheless, if an organization seems to be relieving poverty within a certain group or amongst a certain predefined set of people, the CRA may question whether the purpose of the group is to provide funds to a private group.

The organizations set up to relieve poverty are typically food banks, shelters, and even many missionary groups which provide the basics of life to the poor in developing parts of the world.

Certain other purposes beneficial to the community in a way the law regards as charitable

This heading is not a basket clause to include every other activity that Canadians may want to undertake as registered charities. Rather, it is a broad description of those purposes that do not fall under any of the first three heads but which a court has decided is charitable. There are a number of examples, including hospitals, museums, various children's causes, various seniors' causes, advancing the public's appreciation of the arts, and helping immigrants. There are literally hundreds of years' worth of cases that have been decided all over the Commonwealth and directly affect the types of organizations that may qualify as charitable under this head.

Prospective organizations typically see some other charity operating in this area and understand that they too may qualify. Given that this area of law is often argued by analogy, such reasoning is sound. Clearly, an organization that seeks registration under this head of charity must ask a lawyer with experience in this area to find another case on which the organization can hang its metaphorical hat. You will learn more about this in the section on model objects.

Organizations that seek registration under this head of charity may find the object for which they seek to be organized defined under that section. Assuming that is the case, the work such organizations will have to undertake in order to draft proper objects is already done for them. Therefore, any organization seeking registration in this area may first want to review the model objects put out by the CRA, and, if possible, the objects of other organizations that they intend to emulate.

CRA INTERPRETATIONS

As the development of the law in this area by the courts takes place at a glacial pace (if at all), over the years the CRA has expressed its position on its interpretation of existing law. These interpretations often have the net effect of advancing the law by allowing organizations to engage in activities in ways that would not be clear by a simple reading of the *Income Tax Act* and case law. Any organization seeking registration (or actually operating) in these areas should review the relevant guidance. The CRA currently has published guidance in the following areas:

- Accumulation of property by a public foundation, CPC-005
- Application for relief, CPC-029
- Arts activities and charitable registration, CG-018
- Associated status for unrelated charities, CPC-028
- Attendance at a political fundraising dinner, CPC-001
- Canadian registered charities carrying on activities outside Canada, CG-002
- Charitable organizations outside Canada that have received a gift from Her Majesty in right of Canada, CG-015
- Charitable purposes and activities that benefit youth, CG-020
- Charity's address, CPC-015
- Community economic development activities and charitable registration, CG-014
- Computer-generated official donation receipts, CPS-014
- Donation of gift certificates or gift cards, CG-007
- Expenses incurred by volunteers, CPC-025
- Fair market value of donated item and taxes, CPC-006
- Fundraising by registered charities, CG-013
- General requirements for charitable registration, CG-017
- Gifts of services, CPC-017
- Gifts out of inventory, CPC-018
- Guidelines for the registration of umbrella organizations and title-holding organizations, CPS-026

- Head bodies and their internal divisions, CG-028
- Housing and charitable registration, CG-022
- How to draft purposes for charitable registration, CG-019
- Ineligible individuals, CG-024
- Issuing a receipt in a name other than the donor's, CPC-010
- Management of investment portfolio, CPC-023
- Official donation receipts by a newly registered charity, CPC-009
- Out-of-pocket expenses, CPC-012
- Payment for participation in a youth band or choir, CPC-019
- Political party's use of charity's premises, CPC-007
- Promotion of animal welfare and charitable registration, CG-011
- Promotion of health and charitable registration, CG-021
- Promotion of volunteerism, CPS-025
- Public policy dialogue and development activities by charities, CG-027
- Qualified donees — Consequences of returning donated property, CG-016
- RCAAAs: Receipts-Issuing Policy, CPS-007
- Registered charities making improvements to property leased from others, CPS-006
- Related business and public foundations, CPC-002
- Religious charities — Exemption, CPC-016
- Research as a charitable activity, CPS-029
- Sports and charitable registration, CPS-027
- Third party fundraisers, CPC-026
- Union dues — Payment to a registered charity, CPC-008
- Upholding human rights and charitable registration, CG-001
- Using an intermediary to carry on a charity's activities within Canada, CG-004
- What is a related business?, CPS-019

Copies of all current policies are available at **www.runningacharity.ca**.

PUBLIC BENEFIT

Public benefit has two components. First, if the charity was effective in pursuing its objects, would the result affect a significant segment of the public? Second, would that effect, in fact, be a benefit? Generally, even a cursory review of the proposed charitable object indicates whether there is a benefit intended for a public group (as opposed to a specific family or small religious sect). Even where the intention is to restrict the activities to a minority in the population, certain groups have been found to have been a significant enough section of the population to satisfy the test. For example, many religious groups that qualify as a religion, although a minority in most communities, would still satisfy the public benefit requirement. Other groups may have to prove to the CRA that the people who they wish to benefit, form a significant segment of the community in that area.

The benefit question also cannot be taken for granted. If the CRA does not have prior experience with the type of cause being undertaken, it may seek quantifiable evidence that there is a benefit to the public. The typical example of a situation where the benefit is questionable is where a charity undertakes to create a library in an area so remote it is virtually inaccessible. While clearly a library would be beneficial in an urban area, locating it in a remote rural area where nobody is actually expected to use the library, undermines the benefit.

The CRA may request measurable evidence of the benefit in question, but quantifying benefit can be difficult for a potential organization. In fact, it may be impossible for an organization that has not yet undertaken activities and does not have the resources necessary to do sophisticated market research to prove that their approach meets the public benefit test. Generally, organizations with a novel approach to a community issue are advised to meet with experienced legal counsel prior to submitting their application for charitable status.

MODEL OBJECTS

Perhaps as a measure to increase their own efficiency, but also as a matter of concern for those organizations which seek charitable status, the Charities Directorate put out a list of objects for which they would pre-approve the wording. These objects are known as the model objects and have been expanded once already. The model objects include charitable activities from all of the four different heads and should be reviewed by any organization seeking charitable status prior to submission of an application to the CRA. The current model objects are available in Appendix A. This list will be updated on **www.runningacharity.ca** as the Charities Directorate releases new objects.

DRAFTING OBJECTS

When reviewing the objects drafted by the organization, the CRA looks for three elements. The first element is the charitable category (i.e. the head of charity); the second element is the means of providing the charitable benefit, and the third is the eligible beneficiary group. This type of drafting is rather formulaic and may or may not be in the proposed charity's best interests. While drafting the objects in this manner is not (strictly speaking) necessary to qualify for charitable status, knowing that the Directorate pays special attention to such formulations does tend to help avoid a dispute with the CRA regarding the object's phrasing — if not the actual language.

The first element is often met by including the specific head of charity under which the charity intends to qualify. For example, "to advance education by…" or, "to relieve poverty by…" Where the object in question is the general clause of other activities, one would expect the wording to begin with the specific sub-category such as "to alleviate suffering and distress by…" or "to improve the aesthetic taste of the community by…"

The second element effectively refers to the activities by which the organization wishes to meet its objects. Here, the CRA will be looking for the primary activity or activities that the organization means to undertake to further its objects. For example, operating a food bank, or providing eye surgery. Prospective registrants should know that the information provided with respect to the activities will form the initial judgment of whether the organization is in fact charitable and whether it is formed for the public benefit.

The final element deals with the group of people who are the intended beneficiaries. This is rather self-explanatory, but in terms of developing an object, would effectively circumscribe the people the organization can help. The organization may want to take an expansive view of this, not only because of the CRA's evaluation of the public benefit test, but also so that the organization has room to expand the group of people it wishes to help over time. An example of such a clause is the underlined portion of "to advance health by performing eye surgery for the *poor in El Salvador*" or to "relieve poverty by providing a soup kitchen for the *needy in Calgary*."

BROAD AND VAGUE

One of the CRA's most frequent objections to charitable purposes is that they are both overly broad and vague. Unfortunately, this accusation is hurled with such frequency that it seems clear that the original meaning of the term has been lost to the CRA. An overly broad object is one which allows the charitable organization to undertake non-charitable activities. Moreover, only objects can be overly broad, not activities.

A vague object is one in which it is impossible to tell what the organization intends to do. Broad and vague objects are dealt with in greater detail elsewhere in this book.

DESIGNATION

There are three types of registered charities in Canada: charitable organizations, public foundations and private foundations. Most organizations which intend to undertake activities to further their charitable objects are charitable organizations.

Foundations generally exist to give money to other qualified donees (mostly other registered charities). However, although there are some limitations on foundations which do not exist for charitable organizations, foundations can also undertake their own activities.

Charitable organization

A charitable organization is effectively one which is not controlled by any single individual, group of individuals or entity and which is organized to further its charitable objects through its own charitable activities.

Public foundation

A public foundation is one where control is not exerted by any specific individual or group of individuals who are related to each other. As stated earlier, such organizations typically exist to provide funds to other qualified donees, but may also decide to carry on their own activities.

Private foundation

A private foundation is effectively one where control is exercised by a group of people related to each other. A private foundation is not limited to giving funds to other qualified donees, and can undertake its own charitable activities as well, although this is not usually the case.

Internal CRA designation

The CRA maintains a list of categories in which it places every organization that it registers. This is not the same designation as a charitable organization or foundation as above. Rather, it is internal to the CRA and has no legal meaning at all. Organizations that fall into one category are just as much registered charitable organizations as those in another. The CRA no longer makes the category under which it classifies an organization public. At times, this can become difficult for a group which wants to be registered under one category and be publicly recognized in another. This may happen in the example of an organization that believes itself to be religious, and at the lay sense might very well be, but which cannot be placed into that category because the law simply does not allow for it.

The evidence of the category in which a charity is placed may be found on the CRA's registered charity database under the definition of category. As there is no legal meaning to this designation, it can safely be ignored until such time as the law gives it some meaning.

4 | Registering as a Charity

THE T2050 / T1789 FORM

The key to becoming registered as a charity in Canada is the Application for Registered Charity Status submission to the CRA. The technical CRA designation for this application has been the T2050 form, but the CRA has ceased accepting this form and will instead use a completely online system with the new form T1789. Fundamentally, the reason for the application process is to determine whether the applicant would qualify for registered charity status, so while the form has changed, its purpose has not. A copy of the new form T1789 is on the website **www.runningacharity.ca**.

The application for charitable status will be examined from every angle by the Charities Directorate of the CRA to determine whether the specific applicant organization qualifies for registered charitable status. While the questions may seem innocuous, the CRA will use the form to identify (and will take a strict view) in registering potential charities. As a result, the fact that the form will be compared against the body of charity law to determine whether the applicant will qualify means that there can be tremendous value in having an experienced charity law professional review the form, if not fill it out completely.

The Charities Directorate created a guide for use by lay people when completing the T2050 form. That guide is called the T4063[7]. The new online form T1789 has guidance built into the form itself and has hyperlinks to more detailed guidance, but because of the overlap in the information requested T4063 can still be of use. The guide is an adequate explanation of the information that the Charities Directorate reviews, but it does not explain why the information is being sought so that individuals filling out the form can have some sense of the legal ramifications of their answers. With some understanding of the reason for the question, prospective charities can answer

---

[7] Available at **www.runningacharity.ca**.

more fully and forcefully. At times, we have seen tremendous misunderstandings arise because of approaches taken by different groups in completing the form. This may happen, for example, where a group's religious beliefs are listed in a foreign language or the religious activities, at least superficially, are not put in a religious context.

As the guides are adequate for filling out the forms, this chapter will provide context for the reasons behind the questions being asked. This will help those trying to fill out the application for charitable status on their own to provide the information that the CRA seeks in the manner that it seeks it. This will improve the prospective charity's chances for charitable registration.

ACCESS TO THE CHAMP SYSTEM

At the time of writing the CRA has just unveiled the product of its Charities IT Modernization Project (CHAMP). The charity sector is ripe for this kind of initiative, but it would be euphemistic to suggest that the interface available in mid-2019 is a complete success. As we expect that the CRA will continue to improve and enhance the service, comments made about accessing the system may become outdated. Nevertheless, certain aspects will remain, so these comments may be helpful.

To access the T1789 the organization must have a business number (BN), which usually implies that the organization is a business, but the CRA also assigns these numbers to charities. They are nine digits followed by two letters and then four more numbers. The nine digits identify the entity and the two digits signify the account – RT is for HST, RC is for corporate income tax, and RR is for charities. A typical number might be 12345 6789 RT0001.

Usually, the entity must apply for these numbers from the CRA, although there is a special program that has the CRA automatically issue them to newly created federal corporations. Other societies/not for profit corporations/companies can apply for them through the CRA's Business Registration Online (BRO) or by calling the CRA. Unincorporated organizations and trusts will have a more difficult time because the CRA will only assign the business number to an individual person, and so one of the people involved will have to register. These BNs are all temporary — and the CRA calls those issued to individuals for this purpose such. In all cases, groups that receive charitable registration are assigned new BNs.

The BN allows the prospective registrant to access the CRA's *"My Business Account"*, but don't let the name fool you; it's not just for businesses. The *My Business Account* also asks for more identifying information, all of which should be available to the individual applying for access. This information becomes linked with the individual's personal tax accounts, so sharing access is not a good idea. We understand that the CRA is working on a way for multiple people to access the same charity file through their personal accounts.

Once you are into the *My Business Account*, the T1789 form should be available to the prospective charity. We say 'should' because on the initial rollout of CHAMP it was not linked, and while this glitch is fixed, we do not know if this is permanent. The biggest issue seems to be that the person who fills out the form cannot share a version of it with the other people involved in the charity before submitting it. To date, the CHAMP system does not provide a way of sharing the final version of the form, so only one person can certify its accuracy at the end. This has been a major complaint against the system and we imagine CRA will rectify it as the kinks get worked out.

Section A of T1789 — Identification of the organization

As discussed previously, an organization must be organized as an entity before it can apply for charitable registration. This section of the T2050 form seeks to identify the organization making the application, but the T1789 goes further.

An organization that was previously registered as a charity but lost its registration would also indicate so here. For the sake of clarity, a new organization will have a current name but will not have a previous name or a business number. On the other hand, an organization that has been operating for some time should have a business name and may have previous names by which it was known. It may also have had previous contact with the CRA and/or may be applying for re-registration as a charity.

All organizations will be judged on the record that is presented to the CRA and on information gleaned from internal CRA resources and the Internet. The CRA applies the charity law regime rules to organizations that are seeking registered charity status even though they were not subject to such rules prior to registration. It is therefore easy to understand why a brand new organization may have a better chance at registration than an organization that has been operating for some time. A new organization simply has a cleaner record and less chance that it has fallen offside.

An older organization will have a more difficult time obtaining registered charity status, as will organizations that have already been revoked for cause. Indeed, even some organizations that were revoked for simple failure to file the annual return will find it impossible to be reregistered as a charity. In these cases, the CRA is judging the organization on its previous history, even though it was *not* a charity at the time. Of course, the organization may appeal this decision through the process described in Chapter 7.

At times we have seen situations where prospective charities have applied on their own to the Charities Directorate for registered charity status. The Application was rejected, usually for good reason, because the Applicant did not properly understand the obligations of a charity or the registration system. Applying again, the organization runs the risk of having its past record being applied against it even if the organization manages to clean up its act. It simply may be that the Charities Directorate does not believe that the organization with its new *modus operandi* is substantially different to the one that failed at registration.

In circumstances like this, some groups may abandon the old organization and start afresh with a new organization and a clean record so that there is little confusion as to what this new organization will attempt to accomplish. Again, while the application must be complete and truthful, it is also true that by applying with a clean slate, the organization stands a better chance at being registered as a charity.

The timeliness for considering applications vary depending on the backlog at the Charities Directorate and the staffing situation at the time the application is submitted. In our experience, it takes between six and nine months for an application to be considered and taken to its final determination, depending on the backlog that may exist at the time. There are no firm time commitments from the CRA on processing an application. The Charities Directorate's official position is that it will not expedite any application. But in practice a simpler file, such as a private foundation may be registered more quickly. Also, we have to imagine that, where it is a matter of life and death (such as after a disaster), the CRA may expedite the application so the charity can begin its work. Of course, this does not mean it will register an organization that does not deserve to qualify, so it is still important to structure the organization's affairs in a way that complies with the law and with which the CRA will agree.

The registered office address of the entity is the address at which its books and records will officially be kept. This address will go on file and the CRA will expect that this requirement be followed.

Finally, Part I of the form requests the charity's website, social media accounts and email address. If the charity does not have these in place, it is not compelled to acquire them in order that the CRA may have them.

It is important to note that the CRA will check the publicly available information for evidence that the applicant qualifies for charitable registration. In addition, the CRA will do a Google search of the charity's name and even its directors. Again, while an applicant is not a "charity" and is not subject to the charity rules, the CRA may use whatever it finds on the internet as evidence that the organization would not have qualified if the laws applied to them. It is thus important that the organization review its online content before submitting an application. The review should take into account any factors which the CRA may misunderstand as activities which the organization would inappropriately carry on *after* being granted charitable registration status. Similarly, the organization may wish to make clear any relationships with similar organizations in other countries.

Section C of T1789 — Organizational structure

In the previous chapter, we discussed the different ways in which a corporation can be organized. In Section C of the T1789, the organization provides the necessary information for the Charities Directorate files.

The first question this section asks is whether or not the organization forms the internal division of another organization. Generally speaking, where a corporation has its own governing documents it will not form a subdivision of another organization. This is also true where there exists an umbrella organization of which the applicant is but one of many sister organizations, all with their own incorporating documents.

Where an applicant *is* part of the internal division of another registered charity, the Charities Directorate will require a letter of good standing from the parent organization.

Section D of T1789 — Governing documents

To complete the application for charitable status, the organization must include a copy of its governing documents. This may include a constitution, trust document or (depending on the jurisdiction of the incorporation) letters patent, articles of incorporation or memorandum of association. In addition, if the organization has bylaws and minutes it would be required to forward them.

At times, an organization may register as an unincorporated association and then later incorporate. While we generally discourage organizations from operating in such a way, there are several advantages to registering as an unincorporated organization first. The primary advantage is the cost. It costs very little to set up an unincorporated association and should the applicant fail to achieve registered charity status it can easily unwind such an organization. Furthermore, should the Charities Directorate request any changes to the governing documents, it is a simple matter to amend the governing documents of an unincorporated association. (Conversely, an incorporated entity may require significant documentation, and in the case of an Alberta company, a court order to amend objects.)

Where the group proceeds in this manner, and the Charities Directorate grants registered charity status to an association, the next step is to incorporate a new corporation with the exact same objects as the previous one. The group would then advise the CRA that it has begun carrying out operations as a corporation, and the CRA would transfer the status and issue a new registered charity number to the organization.

Section E of T1789 — Directors and like officials

While this section may seem relatively innocuous in that the questions simply ask for information about the directors or trustees of the organization, there are certain things to keep in mind.

First, all the information is required. If a birth date is missing, the Charities Directorate will return the entire application to you telling you that they need the information. You will then have to seek this information, include it in the form and return the package to the Directorate where it will be returned to the end of the queue.

Second, the information that is included in the form will be used by the CRA for its various purposes. For example, a director that was the director of another charity that has been revoked for cause may disqualify this new organization from charitable registration. The Directorate maintains a list of individuals who are ineligible to serve as directors and will contact you if one of these individuals appears on the new charity roster. Similarly, the Directorate may cross-reference the list of names with other lists that it maintains and return to you with questions or concerns.

The version of the form known as the T1789E (19) asks questions which could be understood as contradictory. Specifically, the form asks for a list of the directors and then asks whether the person is still active or if they resigned from the board. First, past directors have no bearing on whether the Applicant qualifies as a charity, and this is clear overreach by the CRA. Second, an inactive director does not necessarily mean that they resigned. A director who was elected and has not, by operation of law, been removed from that position is still in that position, even if they are not properly conducting their duties. Nevertheless, the Application is clear that the CRA wants to see a list of all prior directors and legal proof that they are no longer such. This may be another good reason to start a new charity from scratch rather than try to collect this information.

This section also asks for information on any other individuals exercising authority over the group, in any capacity. This too is a very broad question, but as it requests information about 'officials' it does not extend to advisors or spiritual leaders who are not *technically* part of the group.

Section F of T1789 — Designation

The differences between Private Foundations, Public Foundations and Charitable Organizations were discussed in an earlier chapter. This section of the T1789 is designed to elicit the information the CRA would need to properly designate the Applicant as one of these. The CRA asks about potential recipients of funds from the Applicant. Technically, it does not matter to which organization the prospective Foundation would give its funds, but as the form does not obligate the Foundation in this way there is no harm in providing the information.

Section G of T1789 — Activities

This part of the application for charitable status is probably the single most important. It should be completed with deliberation and caution, as the Charities Directorate will scour the activities for any indication that the Applicant does not qualify.

Statement of activities

There is no such thing as "charitable activities." Activities cannot be characterized as being charitable or not charitable in and of themselves. The question which must be answered is whether the particular activities further the organization's objects. Of course, that is not to say that any activity which furthers a particular object is necessarily acceptable, but neither is it to say that a particular activity can be judged to disqualify the organization because it doesn't *sound* like something a charity should be doing.

The question that the Charities Directorate must answer is whether the activities further the charitable objects or whether they indicate that the organization has an unstated purpose (particularly a non-charitable one). Of course the additional test is whether the activities somehow put the charity offside the rules of the *Income Tax Act,* any other law or public policy.

The form requests that each activity be listed under the particular charitable object. This is in response to the Charities Directorate's obligation to determine whether the particular activity is in furtherance of that specific object. When describing the activities, keep in mind that the Charities Directorate is looking for evidence of what the charity is doing, how it is doing it and who is benefitting from it. It is important that the explanation be specific and clear. It is also important to remember that the officers of the Charities Directorate are not necessarily experts in the particular area in which the charity will operate. For example, we have dealt with charitable applications on behalf of groups who wish to relieve poverty in distant parts of the world using new technology. The use and applicability of this technology could not reasonably be expected to be known to the charity examiner. It therefore becomes important to explain the nature of the activity and how it furthers the organization's charitable objects.

The application process is hindered by the seemingly endless turnover of staff at the Directorate. Over time one would expect a certain charity examiner to become familiar with, for example, the intricacies of the charities working to preserve the environment. As the turnover is so great, it often happens that just as examiners achieve a level of comfort, they leave the charities examiner role at the CRA.

The applicant must also remember that the Directorate can do their own research. In these circumstances, the Directorate's examiner will use the Internet to dig up additional information on the organization. This often results in confusion because the information on the website is intended for one audience (usually donors) and not contextualized for the CRA. At times, the Directorate's examiner will raise true and critical reasons why the organization does not deserve charitable registration. We commented earlier in this chapter that it is important that the organization review its online content prior to charitable registration, and we reiterate that it is critical that the website reflect the organization's commitment to operating in accordance with charity law.

Organizations often seek to partner with other groups, either foreign or domestic. When applicants plan to work with other organizations, the Directorate will check that the proper legal means by which it can engage in such activities are in place. The Directorate has published guidance on the point which is available at **www.runningacharity.ca**. Operating with a partner in foreign countries is discussed in further detail later in this book.

This section also anticipates that some groups will be created to take over the operations from another organization, particularly ones that are being revoked by the CRA. While this should not matter to a determination of registration, a charity that intends on receiving the assets of a charity that is deregistered will undoubtedly attract greater scrutiny of its directors to determine their relationship to the charity being revoked.

Finally, the section asks about expenses that are not attributable to a charitable activity of the organization. This should be answered very carefully. While there is no specific law on the spending allotments by charities, there is a general rule that all of a charity's assets must be used in the pursuit of charitable activities. The CRA uses this as a license to deny an organization charitable status if too much of its revenue is being used for administrative or fundraising purposes. The CRA's rule-of-thumb is that less than 35% of revenue being used for this purpose will not be investigated; between 35% and 70% will only be justifiable with a sufficient explanation; and more than that will not be allowed.

Section H of T1789 — Gifts and other income generating activities

The first part of this section asks basic questions about the charity's expectations regarding gifts it will receive. For most charities this is an exercise in fantasy, and the CRA knows it. Nevertheless, charities should turn their mind toward the revenue they expect to receive in their first years, and how they expect to attract it. While no justification for the numbers presented must be included, Applicants should try to answer this as honestly as possible.

The rest of this section seeks information relevant to charities regarding related business, tax shelters, and administrative expenses for all forms of revenue generation activity. Applicants considering undertaking such activities should refer to the chapter in this book that discusses the relevant rules and answer the questions accordingly or seek qualified legal counsel to help.

While fundraising expenses are a concern for many Canadians, and the Charities Directorate takes the position that certain levels of fundraising expense are inappropriate, the fact remains that regulating fundraising expense is beyond its jurisdiction. Nevertheless, if the Directorate finds that these expenses are, "too high", it will find some reason to justify denying registration (or revoking the organization's charitable status).

Most organizations have little to fear from questions concerning fundraising expense. Similarly, most organizations that involve the solicitation of donations by volunteers will not concern the Charities Directorate. Organizations that may be involved in business activities to raise funds for their organization should see Chapters 5 and 6.

Section I of T1789 — Political activities

In 2012, the Harper Government gave $8 million to the Charities Directorate to conduct audits of organizations for their involvement in political activity. The fundamental law on the books was not changed; rather it was recognized that charities everywhere on the political spectrum were getting involved in the political process, and some investigation was required to see if they were abiding by the rules.

The audits made clear that the rules regarding political activities for charities were fraught with ambiguity. Consequently, there was an outcry from the charities that were being slated for revocation because the law was simply too vague.

In the 2015 election, the Liberal Party made a change to the political activity rules a plank of their campaign platform, and when they came into power the rules were changed. As expected, the new rules increased the circumstances in which a charity can engage in political activities, and clarified the law to make it easier for charities to remain in compliance.

The new law was rushed through Parliament and passed in December 2018. At the same time, the CRA released a Guidance seeking public input. At the time of writing, the Guidance had not yet been finalized, but will likely be published more or less unchanged from its current form.

POLITICAL ACTIVITIES DEFINED

One of the major critiques of the previous set of rules was that some charities believed that their political purpose could only be accomplished through political means. There-fore, the restriction on the charity from engaging in politics breached the charity's freedom of expression rights under the Charter of Rights and Freedoms. (Indeed, a case went to the Ontario Superior Court and the charity won on these grounds, which was another nail — a big one — in the coffin of the previous set of rules).

The new rules allow a charity to engage in most political activity, so long as it is in pursuit of their charitable objects. For example, a charity that believes that environ-mental conservation is enhanced by banning the use of diesel vehicles can lobby for such a result. Or, if the charity were trying to save lives by promoting a government restriction on certain pesticides, it could put public pressure on the relevant level of government.

It is clearly important then that the charity realize that the activities it wishes to undertake can only be in pursuit of its charitable objects. If for example, the charity is a church and it wishes to engage in political activity relating to the abolition of open pit mining it would have to justify its activities as a pursuit of its objects. In these circumstances, it may simply be safer for the charity to amend its objects to include a more obvious route from the object to the activity.

ALLOWABLE ACTIVITIES

Charities can engage in any activity (except for the ones listed below) designed to change a law, regulation, or policy of a Canadian or foreign government. This is irre-spective of the controversial nature of the change or the practicality of such a change, but must be in furtherance of the organization's charitable objects. Moreover, there is no limit to the amount of resources a charity can use to pursue this change. The major exception to engaging in this activity is that a charity may not engage in *partisan* political activities.

The proposed CRA Guidance considers this a very broad topic. For example, it is clear that a charity could not come out and endorse a specific candidate in any elec-tion, by-election or leadership race, but it should not even engage in activities which may indicate its preference. For example, inviting only a single candidate to come and speak to its members would be a problem, but inviting all candidates would be fine.

There are practical limits to this policy. For example, if the charity supported a certain environmental position and published the voting records of politicians from all parties showing which had voted on similar environmental issues, in the process indicating that one party was in line with its position when others were not, the CRA would deem this to be permissible even though it is implicitly a political endorsement.

At the time of writing CRA's position on the area was still not finalized. A copy of the final guidance is available at **www.runningacharity.ca**.

Sections K, L and M of T1789

The financial information sections of the form requests information to determine if the charity will comply with various technical rules that apply to charities such as private benefit, undue benefit, excess business holding rules, and rules regarding ownership of limited partnerships. However, for most prospective charities, the financial information section is a wild stab in the dark and the more sophisticated rules will not apply. Indeed, if the applicant is indeed involved in some of the more complex financial arrangements, it likely has a lawyer to ensure that they are not falling offside these rules.

Most organizations believe that they are going to raise vast sums for their charitable mission. Undoubtedly this estimation is based on their understanding of the perceived importance of their cause and the assumption that others will agree with them about this importance. However, this ignores the business realities of raising money. In our conversations with the Charities Directorate it is clear that most officers also recognize the futility of seeking realistic estimates from prospective charities. It is thus a wonder that the Directorate still continues to ask for this information, especially as there is no punishment for being honestly wrong about these estimates. Nevertheless, the application form is certified by an officer of the organization, and for that reason (if for no other) the form must be filled out truthfully, and as realistically as possible.

That said, it is best to err on the side of realism as opposed to wild speculation. For example, Section K of the form asks if the applicant has future plans to purchase its own property. One imagines that every charity would answer positively to that question, but without a firm and realistic plan to purchase a property, it is probably more honest to answer in the negative.

Two key elements to keep in mind when completing the proposed budget part of the application is (a) to make sure it is internally consistent and (b) that it considers the ratios of fundraising to spending. Internal consistency refers to the requirement that the numbers have some logic between them. For example, if the organization claims it will only be operating domestically and it reports spending funds abroad, the Directorate will conclude that it is operating internationally. Similarly, while the Directorate will likely take the numbers in a proposed budget with a grain of salt, it will still look at the various ratios to see if the charity is in line with the Directorate's expectations. For example, if the organization intends to spend over 35% of its revenue on fundraising, the Directorate will question whether or not this is appropriate and whether the organization exists to further charitable objects or simply to fund-raise (which is not charitable).

While the CRA's questions are in the nature of one size fits all, applicants should be prepared to answer the question as it applies to them rather than to try and frame an answer that it thinks the CRA wants to hear. For example, the T1789 form hints that a charity must spend every cent of its revenue in a year, but that is not how the law is understood and a prudent organization may well want to save some money for a rainy day. Similarly, the CRA asks for financial statements of organizations that are over one year old, but there is no requirement that unincorporated associations have financial statements. If the CRA insists on some financial information, there is no standard required form for the statements, so it will take the form chosen by the applicant.

On the question of financial information, it is important to take note of the time period used by the form: Section L is prospective for the upcoming year, Section M is as of the date of the application, and Section K has questions in both time periods.

Privacy notice and certification

The nature of the privacy notice is so telling for the CRA's process that it is worth repeating here.

"Personal information is collected under the authority of the *Income Tax Act* and is used to establish and validate the identity and contact information of directors, trustees, officers, like officials, contacts for application purposes, and authorized representatives of the applicant organization. This information will also be used as a basis for the indirect collection of additional personal information from other internal and external sources, which includes personal tax information and relevant financial and biographical information. Personal information will be used to assess the risk of registration with respect to the obligations and requirements as outlined in the Act and the common law.

If the application is approved and the organization is registered, the Canada Revenue Agency (CRA) is permitted to make certain information from the application (including any attachments) and copies of the registration letter (including any conditions and warnings contained therein) available to the public, with the exception of information marked as confidential. If registration is denied, the information will not be provided to the public. Personal information may also be disclosed to the applicant organization, contacts for application purposes and authorized representatives, as well as other government agencies and departments under information-sharing agreements, and in accordance with section 241 of the Act. Incomplete or inaccurate information may result in the Charities Directorate not processing the application or may result in a refusal to register.

Personal information is described in personal information bank CRA PPU 200 and is protected under the Privacy Act. Individuals have a right of protection, access to and correction or notation of their personal information. You are entitled to complain to the Privacy Commissioner of Canada regarding our handling of your information.

Notification to directors and like officials: The CRA strongly encourages the applicant organization to voluntarily inform its directors and like officials that it has collected and disclosed their personal information to the CRA."

The term "confidential" is awkward given that *all* the information the form requests would seem to be confidential. The reason for the clarification of the term is that the rest of the form may become available to the public, and for reasons of security and some degree of privacy, the Directorate agrees to keep certain information confidential.

Certification

The application form must be certified as accurate prior to submission. Under the CHAMP system as it exists currently, only one person is required to digitally certify the document, and it cannot be reviewed by any others. This will surely be changed as the system evolves. To our knowledge nobody has ever been penalized for falsely certifying the contents of an application for registered charity status, but the individual directors who are certifying the form should take it seriously, even if there is no real possibility of punishment for errors made.

POST-APPLICATION PROCESS

Once the application form is submitted to the Charities Directorate it will be reviewed first by a front-line person to determine that the application is complete.

Once the CRA confirms that the application is complete it will be assigned a file number. A letter indicating the file number will be forwarded to the applicant's contact person or authorized representative. Then, depending on the backlog at the CRA, the application will be reviewed by the examiner and a decision will be made about its treatment. The usual options in this case are to register the applicant as a charity or to respond with a letter requesting further information. In some circumstances, the Directorate will agree to register the organization if certain changes are made in the applicant's objects or governing documents.

Assuming all the requirements are met, the notification of registration will be sent to the organization, and it may begin its charitable operations using the business number included on that paper.

If the organization receives a "Notice of Refusal of Registration" it may begin the dispute process resolution described in Chapter 8.

PART II

MAINTAINING A CHARITY

———

5 | Books and Records

INTRODUCTION

The rules discussed in this book are of limited value if they can't be enforced. Given that our tax system is one of honest compliance, the laws can only be enforced retroactively through a review of the books and records made available to the CRA. For this reason, keeping proper books and records is in itself a requirement under the *Income Tax Act*. The main requirement is that a charity have sufficient books and records to show that it is in compliance with the law. Unfortunately, as it is impossible to prove that you have enough books and records, the CRA can, with few restrictions, almost always allege that there are insufficient books and records.

Nevertheless, given that the CRA can only judge an organization on the evidentiary record placed before it, it is imperative that charities understand the legal requirements, and do their best to maintain proper records.

WHAT ARE BOOKS AND RECORDS?

As a general rule, the CRA does not stipulate the types of books and records an organization must keep. Fundamentally, however, an organization must have sufficient evidence to show that it is in compliance with the Act. To be clear, destroying evidence that an organization is not in compliance will not help the organization, as the lack of documents is, in itself, an offence. (Although the documents could be evidence of an offence with a more grievous penalty.) And, lack of documentation could become a problem if the CRA suspects that an organization is non-compliant due to lack of documents, but the organization has no evidence to demonstrate that it is in compliance with the Act.

There is a difference between the two concepts of 'books' and 'records'. 'Books' is not a defined term in the *Income Tax Act* but is typically understood to be accounting records. A 'record' is defined and includes "an account, an agreement, a book, a charter table, a diagram, a form, an image, an invoice, a letter, a map, a memorandum, a plan, a return, a statement, a telegram, a voucher, and any other thing containing information whether written or in any other form." Surprisingly, this definition is not exhaustive and, in fact, if there are other types of records that exist they would be included as well.

No distinction is made in law between *corporate* and *transactional* records, but in practice there is a difference. Corporate records are those documents required by law to define a corporation and its governance. They are often created with the co-operation of a government office and are required so that the corporation meets certain statutory requirements. Transactional records are those created by the organization to keep track of its operations and meetings. They still help the corporation meet its requirements under the law, but if the meetings did not occur or records were not kept of meetings, the corporation and its governance would still exist.

CORPORATE RECORDS

A corporate entity must maintain current copies of its constituting documents (Articles of Incorporation, Articles of Continuance, Letters of Patent, Supplementary Letters of Patent, etc.), bylaws and minutes of meetings or resolutions. Organizations operating in more than one province would also be expected to have copies of their extra-provincial registration.

Meetings

Compliance with the various corporate acts requires minutes of meetings of both directors and members. While most statutes only require that the members have an annual general meeting, directors generally meet more often and should have records of all of their formal meetings. Directors may also have informal meetings where matters are discussed between two or more of the directors. While there is no corporate requirement to maintain records of these meetings, if an organization effectively operates though this method of informal meeting, the CRA may request to see copies of these records; unless there is some other decision-making method it would be appropriate to keep such records.

From time to time the CRA uses the records to opine on topics which are technically beyond its jurisdiction. For example, we have seen instances where the CRA opines on the internal controls that a charity uses. There is no law that requires a charity to use one method or another, but the CRA will often interpret its role broadly to ensure a charity's assets are properly used. Consequently, even if the charity comes to a different conclusion than the CRA would like to see, the fact that it had the discussion is in itself valuable and it would be unwise for a charity to self-censor its minutes before releasing to the CRA.

Format

There is no specific requirement that the record of happenings at meetings be kept in any particular way for the CRA's purposes (although for purposes of consistency, groups may wish to follow standard processes). Therefore, meetings that simply have notes of what was said and confirmed as accurate by the bulk of the attendees at the meeting are sufficient for the CRA's purposes. It is important nonetheless to understand the information that the CRA seeks in these records. This will depend on the nature of the offence they are investigating. For example, if they are looking to see that books and records are maintained, then the existence of the record alone is sufficient; if they are seeking to know if control and direction is exercised over charity assets, they will look for evidence that the board discusses these issues and actually asserts control; if they are investigating related business issues, they may wish to understand the relative amount of board time that is dedicated to managing the business. But as all of these reviews are conducted retroactively, it is important to record discussions as they occur because you cannot know what the CRA will later seek.

Corporate bylaws do follow a general format and have certain requirements based on the jurisdiction in which the organization is incorporated. They will often deal with the admission of members, the calling of meetings, and the appointment of officers — to name a few areas. They may also deal with issues of specific concern to the corporation that are not strictly required by the relevant corporate law, such as a relationship to a parent body or discipline of members. Copies of sample minutes for meetings of members and directors can be obtained on **www.runningacharity.ca**.

Corporate records are among the most difficult for charities to maintain. They require compliance with at least one set of corporate statutes and perhaps more. They follow a technical format and involve filings with various government ministries. They also involve up-to-date registers of members and directors and records of director meetings. We would suggest that charities contact a lawyer experienced with minutes for charitable corporations in order that the legal components be satisfied on a yearly basis.

TRANSACTIONAL RECORDS

The vast majority of records held by a charity are its 'transactional' records. They are created by the day-to-day transactions of the organization and include its bank account statements, cheques, records of employee payment, invoices, statements of account, deposit books, etc, these are generally easy records for the organization to obtain as they are created by third parties. The challenge for most charities is to organize these records into some logical format in order that their T3010 can be produced at the end of the year. This role generally falls to a bookkeeper or some other individual prepared to keep these records.

On the assumption that the bulk of these records are being created by a third party, and that the charity simply needs to keep them, the charity will not face any difficulty in ensuring that its transactions are properly maintained. However, there are situations in which a charity faces difficulties because it is in a non-commercial or non-traditional setting.

Charities that engage in relief of poverty may find it difficult to track the expenditures with which they give alms to the poor. This can be obvious in a situation where the charity distributes food to individuals that simply need it or seem to need it. While the CRA is obviously aware that a charity is engaged in the provision of food for the hungry it may ask how it can be certain that food is being given only to the poor and is not, for example, being distributed to the employees of the organization or being sold. While the CRA can be forgiving in such situations, it can in some cases be extremely difficult to ensure that records are maintained so as to show that the charity's resources are being properly used. At times we have suggested that charities avoid this work and seek to support the poor in a way that can be documented. Or, at least, the food received could be accepted by way of signature of the recipient.

Foreign countries present an additional problem in that often the normal transactional records we would expect in Canada, say on the purchase of office supplies, simply may not exist there. Receipts and invoices are simply not used in some parts of the world. A recent decision of a Tax Court Judge suggested simply having a notebook where the purchase is acknowledged by signature of the vendor. It is unclear whether or not the CRA would accept this as sufficient, but it meets the definition of a record and may be acceptable.

In these non-traditional circumstances, the charity must simply do the best it can to document that its resources are being properly used. In these circumstances, charities must be creative in order to ensure that the CRA can see the organization is in compliance with its obligations.

Additional records

Additional records are those records which come into the organization's possession or which are created by the organization and are not either its corporate records or transactional records. These may include emails, or letters to the organization — and they may include records that the organization purposely creates in order that the CRA, if it ever looks to see, will accept as proof that the organization is properly meeting its responsibilities.

Emails to and from the organization and letters to the organization must clearly be maintained. Less clear are letters and emails written by volunteers from their personal email accounts regarding organization business. Obviously, if a volunteer writes an email to an official of the organization, those records become part of the charity's overall books and records, but emails between volunteers about charity business are not clearly part of the books and records of the organization, and may not even be known by officials of the charity. If the CRA were to request books and records showing control and direction (for example) over an activity of the organization, the charity may choose to seek out additional records from its volunteers.

An official of the charity using his or her personal email account in order to conduct business of the charity may be unable to claim privacy over these emails. A director acting in such capacity, dealing with affairs of the organization has arguably created a record of the organization and should consider providing a copy for the official records. Clearly, this can be a difficult undertaking and can be made much more efficient through the use of email accounts belonging to the organization only. As these are relatively easy to create, it makes sense for an individual to do this to clearly separate their role in acting for the charity versus their private role.

Creating records

The organization may also seek to create records where otherwise none previously would have existed. This would be the case where an organization wants to demonstrate, for example, control and direction over the use of its resources. In a circumstance where the organization uses an agent to operate abroad, having an agency agreement may not be sufficient. The organization may seek statements regarding the use of its resources from officials of the agent and it may create written records of site visits by the charity, including photographic or video evidence of the happenings abroad.

The same might be true in circumstances where the organization is operating a related business. In these circumstances the organization may wish to create records to show that, in fact, the role of the business is still subordinate to the organization's overall charitable purposes. The point is that, even in circumstances which would otherwise go undocumented, the organization may want to document them specifically to create a record should the CRA later investigate. Given that the CRA alleges with regularity that an organization has insufficient books and records to show that it is in compliance with the Act, this should actually be top-of-mind for administrators.

To properly create a paper trail, the charity must have a good idea of what it wishes to demonstrate. This in turn, is based on an understanding of the legal requirements in any situation. To ensure that a charity's resources are properly used, the organization must make certain that the records show the organization used its resources solely on its own activities, and that it has control and direction over those activities. If there could be any question about whether or not the charity has control and direction over those resources, as may happen if there is a third party involved, the charity should create records to show that it has that control and direction.

Further, if an organization loans its assets to a third party, the organization should have proper loan arrangements documented so that the CRA understands this is not a gift of its assets but rather a loan. If an organization is involved in advocacy it will be important for the organization to create a written record, if only for its own records, to show that the content of the advocacy was in compliance with the Act.

Fundamentally, it is important that a charity understand what it must show in its records in order to comply with the law should the CRA investigate (hence the rest of this book). Continuous education regarding a charity's obligations is critical so that the administration of the organization understands when to ask for reports of directors or others in whatever circumstances. As this is often too onerous a task for most administrators, charities should get into the habit of constantly producing reports by various parties and keeping them on file should the CRA ever wish to see them.

WHERE MUST THEY BE KEPT?

The books and records of an organization must be kept, by law, at its registered office address. This however, is often an impossible task because the Corporate Records may be more easily kept at a lawyer's office, accounting records may be with the accountant, and other records may be with the organization. It can be inconvenient and costly to keep all the records in one place — particularly if they are voluminous.

The CRA, to our knowledge, has never insisted on the requirement that an organization keep all its books and records at the registered office address. It understands the practical difficulties and has never sought to confirm the particular location of these records. In the course of an audit, CRA auditors generally either ask for information to be provided to them or meet at a mutually convenient location where the records are produced. Nevertheless, we have seen instances where charities lose track of the location of their documents and so it would be wise for an organization to be aware of its records should they have to be produced.

ELECTRONIC RECORD KEEPING

Nowadays, more and more records are either created in paper format for conversion to electronic format or in electronic format able to be printed at any time. Obviously, the CRA is as much interested in easy record-keeping as anybody else, and rules do exist for doing so electronically. These rules are outlined in two technical documents from the CRA, IC78-10R5 and IC 05-1R1. Both are available on **www.runningcharity.ca**.

An organization that keeps electronic records must be able to provide them in an electronically readable and useable format to the CRA auditors so that they can be read on CRA equipment (although not every CRA department will accept electronic documents). For most modern records this is not an issue, as long as they can be produced in PDF format. A regular problem is that the organization uses a bookkeeping or accounting software unknown to the CRA. However, as these records can often be converted from one format to another, there is usually a work-around. Electronic files can be encrypted, but the password must be provided to the CRA if requested.

If a record was originally created in paper format and then converted to electronic, the paper does not need to be kept. However, an electronic record must always be kept, even if converted from one format to another.

The CRA does allow for the keeping of these records online in the cloud. However, their requirement is that the server be located in Canada or at least that a copy of the records be maintained on a server in Canada.

One difficulty that arises from time to time — and it does not apply only to electronic records — is the accidental destruction of records. With paper records this can happen in terms of a fire or some other disaster, but with electronic records the loss of a USB key could undermine years of work by the organization. For this reason, electronic records should be copied and kept in safe, redundant, locations as much as possible. If records are lost, the CRA may seek proof or a reason for such a loss and may be forgiving in the circumstance. However, there's no guarantee that the CRA will take this approach, and you can assume that the CRA auditors have heard the "dog ate my homework" type of excuse more often than most teachers.

HOW LONG TO KEEP RECORDS

Generally speaking, all books and records must be kept be for a minimum of six years from the end of the last tax year from which they relate. The tax year end is the same as the fiscal year end for the corporation, but is, by definition, the calendar year end for trusts and unincorporated associations. For purposes of the Employment Insurance Act and the Canada Pension Plan Act, the retention period begins at the end of the calendar year to which the books and records relate. Technically, duplicate donation receipts of a registered charity (other than receipts for donations of property, which may be held for longer periods of time) is two years from the end of the calendar year in which the donations were made — but it would be inadvisable for a charity to rely on this specific requirement rather than the general one.

The obligations above relate to the *Income Tax Act*, but it is important to understand that obligations also exist in the various corporate acts. Typically, Corporate Records (as opposed to Transactional Records) are not destroyed. For example, it is important to remember in charitable corporations the directors admit the members and the members elect the directors, so the chain of authority begins with the actual original incorporation. The original group eventually moves on and the people that took over then have the power to elect the new directors, but of course, if those people were never properly admitted or if the newer directors were never elected by people with the legal authority to do so, the chain of authority has been lost. The same situation exists if the corporation does not have records to prove this legal 'chain'.

There are other situations in which books and records could be useful and destroying them prematurely could have an adverse effect on the charity. For example, donors may be in a position that their receipts are being challenged and therefore, the records of their donation held by the charity could be useful. Another situation could arise when the charity has been involved in a project that resulted in some lengthy ongoing litigation (perhaps a construction accident or in historical cases of abuse). In these cases the litigation timeline can go beyond the legal requirements of keeping records, and the charity may need its records from a far-earlier time period.

Those charities operating overseas may also be subject to document retention periods covering their periods of operation abroad.

Records of dissolved corporations must still be kept for an additional two years after the date of dissolution, and for registered charities which have lost their status, records must be kept for two years from the date of revocation of registration. Notwithstanding these technical requirements, on a practical level, records should be kept much longer. Remember that if the CRA decides to audit an organization, it is up to the organization to prove that it has complied with the law. If the organization or its donors were to end up at the Tax Court the burden of proof is generally on the individual or charity to prove compliance with the law. Therefore, it can be a good insurance policy to keep records for significantly longer than the six-year requirement.

Destroying records to save space was much more of an issue when electronic records were less ubiquitous. Now that electronic records are created as a matter of course in the first instance and paper records can easily be converted to electronic records, there is no reason why records cannot be kept indefinitely.

WHO CAN SEE RECORDS

Outside of the civil litigation in which a plaintiff or defendant could be compelled to produce documents relating to the litigation, there are really three groups of individuals who may be able to see various parts of corporate records. They are the directors, the members and government officials. In circumstances of litigation, an opposing party may be able to force the charity to produce records. Here, we are concerned with the CRA.

Directors

Under most of the corporate laws relevant to corporations without share capital, a corporation must keep records containing the following:

a) Any articles, bylaws and amendments;

b) Minutes of meetings of members or committees of members;

c) Resolutions of members or committees of members;

d) Any debt obligations issued by the corporation;

e) A directors registry;

f) An officers registry;

g) A members registry;

As a general rule, directors are entitled to see all the records that are in the corporation that go back to any point in the corporation's history.

While the corporate law does not extend this right to the financial information, as part of the mind and management of the organization, a director would not be properly exercising his or her authority without a periodic review of the financial records. A director of the corporation should be entitled to see these records whenever they may see fit.

Members

The right of members to see corporate records is a bit more restricted and is determined by the relevant law under which the organization was constituted. As Trusts have no members, this concept is not applied to a Trust; neither does it apply to an unincorporated association which may refer to certain people as members but who do not technically have that distinction. Different statutes have different provisions allowing members to see the corporate records. These rights are generally limited to the list of seven categories listed above, and therefore exclude most financial records. To access these financial records, a member would need to investigate the appropriate statute and consider making a request of the appropriate government department to allow for a special right to review all of the accounting records. Review of the seven categories mentioned above is usually allowed as a right, but the *use* of the information is limited. Typically the information can only be used to allow for the members to request a members meeting or to contact the members for purposes of corporate business. The intention is not to allow the individual to use the list for any personal means.

Government investigators/auditors

There may be any number of government departments that could require a corporation to provide copies of its records. Typically, this would be limited to the areas of interest of the particular government department. For example, a city department licensing daycares may seek to know who the directors of the corporation are to ensure that there are no impediments to the directors working with children, but the membership of the corporation is unnecessary for this purpose.

Generally, the government department responsible for corporations retains the power to investigate all aspects of the corporation to ensure that it is compliant with the law and in the case of charities, that charitable property is protected.

By far though, it is the CRA that has the greatest powers of investigation into a charity's records. While most government departments are limited to the areas of specific interest, the CRA has wide powers to compel the production of any document at all, of any type, and indeed even recordings which may not be documents at all in order to investigate the corporation. Indeed, as Canada does not have a regulator of charities with the power to investigate all aspect of a charity's operation, it is the CRA that, by default, exercised this power.

Generally speaking, when the CRA audits an organization, it will begin with a polite request to produce the requested documents. If the organization refuses to do so, the CRA could produce a formal document demanding under law, with penalty of prosecution, that the documents be produced. There are times, when this is the right course of action and the charity may require the CRA to legally demand it. This may be in circumstances where the charity does not want to be accused by donors or members of working with the CRA to their detriment. In this case, the charity may want the cover of legal demand before producing the documentation.

In certain circumstances, the charity may still refuse to provide certain documents protected by privilege. For example, solicitor-client privilege. There is specific process by which this is handled, requiring review by a judge. Given the potential consequences of a refusal to provide information to the CRA, a lawyer be consulted if the charity believes there are any documents that may be a breach of privilege or privacy to produce. The law regarding privilege is vast and ancient, and involves statements made to doctors or priests as well as lawyers (but not accountants), and includes situations where documents are prepared specifically for litigation. Only an experienced lawyer can guide an organization through this process.

WHAT LANGUAGE

The law requires that books and records be kept in either English or French. Presumably, an organization cannot be penalized for keeping them in both interchangeably.

Organizations that operate overseas typically have records in another language, and while technically the organization should have them translated as they are produced, practically this is often an unnecessary expenditure. While the CRA's audit procedures limit an audit to a certain number of years, translating every document as it comes through may be unnecessary for years that not under audit. Even for years under audit, the CRA at times requests just sample documents, so translating every document is may not be necessary.

Generally, the CRA allows a period of time for the production of documents and understands that organizations operating in non-English or French-speaking parts of the world will have documents in other languages. Indeed, if someone sends an email to an organization in a language that is not English the organization can hardly be faulted for the fact that its books and records are in English or French. In these circumstances, the organization will usually have to act quickly to translate the documents, and while this may introduce some bursts of costs it is often the only practical way to deal with non-English or French materials economically and efficiently.

CREATING BOOKS AND RECORDS

We have discussed earlier in this chapter about records that are automatically created and records that the organization should, on a continuous basis, go out of its way to create to document its files. However, often when the CRA requests records the charity is at a loss because it simply does not have them.

The law does not require an organization to create records that it does not have. It does require it to maintain sufficient books records to demonstrate that it is complying with the law. Nonetheless, it is usually unwise and unnecessary for a charity to create records because the CRA has requested them. At best this is documenting retrospectively what had previously occurred, and usually this is not done properly. Indeed, we have had clients threatened by the CRA that they would take our documents for forensic analysis to determine the general timing in which the document was produced (an unnecessary and unkind remark).

If the organization has information which is relevant for the audit, it can be provided to the CRA either by way of letter or verbally. If the organization can reasonably produce records that reflect what had previously happened, there is nothing which precludes it from doing that (but the document date should reflect its production date), again this must be done with caution and an eye to the legal requirements. One example are corporate records. Corporations often forget to prepare their annual general meeting documents or the documents reflecting the admittance of members.

Meeting auditors

Audits often begin with an interview by the auditor of the representative of the organization, and these meetings can result in misunderstandings and miscommunication. Convincing an auditor that they misunderstood can be next to impossible and may require a judge to, in fact, hear testimony in order to get a different take on those comments.

While this can occur to anyone, and native English speakers can use the same term in different ways creating confusion, the problem is exacerbated by individuals whose English is not their first language (this applies both to representatives of the charity and of the CRA).

This problem is often ameliorated if the conversation can be recorded and transcript can be produced, or the recording otherwise reviewed to determine if there was a misunderstanding. However, the current CRA policy does not allow their auditors to be recorded, so it is wise to have an outside party attend and take notes of the meeting and perhaps, interject when they think some term or concept is being misunderstood by one or the other party.

The other alternative is to simply to refuse to meet with the CRA. While the auditor will likely be indignant and insist that they have the legal authority to compel attendance at an interview, in fact there are limits to their authority and at times cannot do so without a subpoena.

Individuals and charities are often afraid of subpoenas, but they are nothing more than a requirement to attend (albeit with legal consequences for non-attendance). There is no reason that the CRA should refuse to record their conversations, and if this is the kind of action needed to ensure that the charity and its donors are protected, then so be it.

PUNISHMENTS

Various punishments exist for non-production or inadequate production of books and records. Generally, with respect to charities the CRA will either prepare a compliance agreement or otherwise revoke the organization's charitable status. In theory, there are additional punishments that may arise, and while there are provisions in the *Income*

Tax Act that in theory could allow for imprisonment for non-production of records, this is unlikely unless criminal behaviour is involved.

There are other applicable acts, most notably the various corporate acts under which the organization may be set up. These acts also provide for punishments up to dissolution of the organization if there are inadequate books and records.

6 | Raising Funds

Convincing a donor to make a gift to a charity is partly an appeal to the individual's sense of altruism and partly a practical discussion of the cost of the gift to the donor. Therefore, to effectively solicit a donation, the prospective donee must have a good working knowledge of the cost of the donation to the donor — the object, of course, being to maximize the size of the donation and minimize its cost. To paraphrase Jean-Baptiste Colbert in his famous statement about taxation, the art of fundraising consists in so plucking the goose as to get the most feathers with the least hissing.

Since donations to registered charities are given a special tax treatment, the actual cost to the donor must be determined with reference to the *Income Tax Act* (ITA). Unfortunately, the ITA is a huge, unwieldy and extremely technical document not designed for casual reference. To make matters worse, the after-tax cost to the donor may depend on the item donated (and in some cases, on who is the recipient of the gift). This chapter is designed to give readers an understanding of the after-tax cost of donations to donors, as a means to improve fundraising efforts and ultimately increase the amount of donations coming into the organization.

While *Part I — Starting a Charity* discusses the basic tax concepts necessary to understand some of the more complex issues in this chapter, a small review is worthwhile. Canada has a progressive income tax structure, which means that as income rises, so does the tax rate on the next dollar. For example, all other things being equal, everyone in the same jurisdiction would pay the same tax on their first $35,000 of taxable income Those who earn more than $35,000 would pay a higher rate on their next $35,000 of taxable income (or any portion thereof), and so on. When income is earned in a year, it is generally taxable. So, if an individual receives $1,000 from her employer, she is taxed on $1,000.

Similarly, there are tax consequences if an individual sells or donates a piece of property. If the item is inventory in a business for that individual, the profits of the sale or donation are considered income and treated in the same manner as if they had been paid by an employer. On the other hand, if the donor owns the property to earn income from it, but not through the sale of it, it is generally considered a piece of capital property.

Example:

Asher has a stock portfolio but does not engage in heavy trading and holds them to earn dividend income. He likely owns the shares as *capital property*, whereas Ezra earns his daily living from the appreciation in value on shares and therefore likely holds his shares as *inventory*. When a piece of capital property is eventually sold, the owner is generally taxed on the gain in value that occurred while he or she owned that particular item. This is called a capital gain, and only 50% of it is taxable. If a capital item decreases in value while held by the owner, it is a capital loss and is not taxable.

The tax consequence of a sale or gift (called a disposition) is the single biggest factor affecting the cost of a donation. Thus, a familiarity with these rules is crucial to raising significant donations.

DONATION OF INCOME VS. CAPITAL		
	Income	Capital
Amount of donation	$1,000	$1,000
Taxable amount	$1,000	$500
Sample tax rate	46%	46%
Tax owing	$460	$230

After the amount of tax owing is calculated, tax credits are subtracted from this amount to determine the total amount payable. Notably, if nothing is owing, non-refundable tax credits do not result in a payment to the taxpayer. Donations by individuals result in non-refundable tax credits. The tax credit itself is determined by multiplying the first $200 by the lowest combined federal/provincial rate in the appropriate province (except Alberta), and multiplying everything over $200 by the designated rate (in most Canadian jurisdictions the highest rate). The following table illustrates the tax credits available for donations of $1,200 in the different provinces.

Tax credit on $1,200 in donations for 2019

Province	Combined federal/ provincial tax credit rate on first $200 donation	Tax credit	Combined federal/ provincial tax credit rate on amounts over $200[8]	Tax credit on amount over $200	Total combined federal and provincial tax credit
Alberta[9]	25.00%	$50.00	54.00%	$540.00	$590.00
British Columbia	20.06%	$40.12	49.80%	$498.00	$538.12
Manitoba	25.8%	$51.60	50.4%	$504.00	$555.60
New Brunswick	24.68%	$49.36	50.95%	$509.50	$558.86
Newfoundland	23.70%	$47.40	51.3%	$513.00	$560.40
Northwest Territories	20.90%	$41.80	47.05%	$470.50	$512.30
Nova Scotia	23.79%	$47.58	54.00%	$540.00	$587.58
Nunavut	19.00%	$38.00	44.50%	$445.00	$483.00
Ontario[10]	20.05%	$40.10	44.16%	$441.60	$481.70
Prince Edward Island[11]	24.80%	$49.60	49.70%	$497.00	$546.60
Saskatchewan	25.50%	$51.00	47.50%	$475.00	$526.00
Yukon	21.40%	$42.80	45.80%	$458.00	$500.80

To simplify the discussion, this chapter will make several assumptions. First, unless otherwise stated, the donor holds the items to be donated as capital property. Second, we will assume a credit rate of 46%.

---

[8] For the sake of simplicity we assume the highest Federal tax bracket, but even if the individual was in the second-highest bracket the credit rate would drop down to offset the tax owing in that bracket.

[9] The tax credit for donations over $200 more than offsets the taxes that would otherwise have been due.

[10] When the provincial surtaxes are taken into account, the offset at the highest marginal rates is somewhat higher.

[11] As PEI charges surtaxes when provincial tax exceeds $12,500, the effect of the offset is higher with income over approximately $99,000 (assuming a single individual with only the basic personal exemption).

DONATIONS OF CASH

Donations of cash are fairly straightforward. The charity simply receipts the face value of the amount donated. (This does not apply to currency held for collection purposes). Assuming that the donor earned that cash in the same year it was donated, then tax would otherwise have to be paid on it (ignoring for a moment the practical issue that taxes on employment income are generally deducted at the source). Depending on the province and the donor's tax bracket, the tax credits generated from the donation would offset the tax owing on the income earned, so no tax would be payable on the money earned — and then donated. At lower income brackets, and in Alberta, the credits would actually more than offset the tax owing and the donor would be able to shelter other income from tax with the credits earned from this donation. If the donor is donating cash that is not income to him in the year donating, the credit could be used to offset taxes owing from other sources. But in those provinces where the tax rate is higher than the credit rate on donations, the donor could still be paying tax on a dollar given to charity!

PUBLIC SECURITIES

As discussed, Canada has a capital gains tax that is levied on 50% of the *appreciation in value* of the capital good.[12] The tax is levied when the item is disposed of (i.e. sold or given away). In most circumstances, it is irrelevant whether the asset is sold or donated. However, the ITA does contain an exemption for certain capital assets donated to a registered charity such as publicly-listed securities donated to charity (note that this does not include shares held in an RRSP, RRIF, or pension plan). Moreover, the donor continues to receive a donation tax receipt equal to the fair market value of the shares donated. Thus, there is no tax on the donation, but the donor still receives a tax credit equal to the fair market value of the donation.

A publicly-listed security is effectively any share listed on a number of exchanges throughout the world. This list of exchanges is defined by regulation and changes from time to time. As of January 2019 the list includes:

- Canada: Aequitas NEO Exchange
- Canada: Canadian National Stock Exchange (operating as the Canadian Securities Exchange)
- Canada: Montreal Exchange
- Canada: TSX Venture Exchange (Tiers 1 and 2)
- Canada: Toronto Stock Exchange
- Australia: Australian Securities Exchange

---

[12] See Chapter 1 for a discussion of capital vs. income.

- Austria: Vienna Stock Exchange
- Belgium: Euronext Brussels
- Bermuda: Bermuda Stock Exchange
- Brazil: BM&F Bovespa Stock Exchange
- Czech Republic: Prague Stock Exchange (Prime Market)
- Denmark: Nasdaq Copenhagen
- Finland: Nasdaq Helsinki
- France: Euronext Paris
- Germany: Frankfurt Stock Exchange
- Germany: Boerse Stuttgart AG (Stuttgart Stock Exchange)
- Hong Kong: The Hong Kong Stock Exchange
- Ireland: Irish Stock Exchange
- Israel: Tel Aviv Stock Exchange
- Italy: Borsa Italiana S.p.A (Milan Stock Exchange)
- Jamaica: Jamaica Stock Exchange (Senior Market)
- Japan: Tokyo Stock Exchange
- Luxembourg: Luxembourg Stock Exchange
- Mexico: Mexico City Stock Exchange
- Netherlands: Euronext Amsterdam
- New Zealand: New Zealand Stock Exchange
- Norway: Oslo Stock Exchange
- Poland: The main and parallel markets of the Warsaw Stock Exchange
- Republic of Korea: Korea Exchange (KOSPI and KOSDAQ)
- Singapore: Singapore Stock Exchange
- South Africa: Johannesburg Stock Exchange
- Spain: Bolsa de Madrid (Madrid Stock Exchange)
- Sweden: Nasdaq Stockholm
- Switzerland: SWX Swiss Exchange
- United Kingdom: London Stock Exchange
- United States: BATS Exchange

- United States: Nasdaq BX

- United States: Chicago Board of Options

- United States: Chicago Board of Trade

- United States: Chicago Stock Exchange

- United States: National Association of Securities Dealers Automated Quotation System (Nasdaq)

- United States: National Stock Exchange

- United States: New York Stock Exchange

- United States: NYSE Arca

- United States: NYSE MKT

- United States: Nasdaq PHLX

Example:

Assume that Nell lives in Ontario and buys one share of a high-tech company for $1.00. Over time, the share rises in value and may even split once or more than once. After ten years, with all splits factored in, Nell owns shares worth a total of $100. If Nell were to sell the share she would have a capital gain of $99 (i.e. the fair market value of $100, less the cost of $1). Applying the capital gains inclusion rate of 50%, only $47.50 would be taxable. Further applying a tax rate of 46% the amount of tax payable would be $21.85. Thus, if Nell sells the shares she is left with after-tax income of $78.15 (i.e. $100 – $21.85).

Conversely, let's say Nell decides she wants to donate her shares instead of selling them. In this case, Nell has no tax to pay and of course, receives no income from the sale of the shares. She does however receive a tax receipt for $100, which will offset $46 of taxes due from other sources. So, assuming Nell is paying tax on income from other sources, the actual after-tax cost of this donation is $54.

FLOW-THROUGH SHARES

Flow-through shares are defined in extremely technical language in the *Income Tax Act*, but are fairly easy to understand. Generally speaking, the ITA imposes tax on the amount of income earned by a taxpayer, less any amounts deducted. Expenses incurred to earn income are deductible. However, one can only deduct these expenses from income earned; if no income is earned, the deductions are lost.

Mining companies incur significant expenses before they create a revenue stream. So, in order to encourage investment in the mining sector, the federal government basically allows the owner of a flow-through share to deduct expenses incurred by the mining company from his or her personal income. Depending on whether the expense incurred is in the exploration phase or the development phase (of a mine or similar process), the expenses are deductible at a rate of either 100% or 30%, respectively. To make things even better, the federal government has provided a "super flow-through" credit of 15%, which it tends to renew in each federal budget.

The catch is that, for income tax purposes, the cost of the share is deemed to be zero. So even if the buyer buys the share at $10.00 and sells it at $8.00, the share is still assumed to have gained $8.00 in value and is therefore taxed on an $8.00 capital gain even though it actually lost $2.00. Of course, given that the shareholder will have already deducted the 'flowed-through' expenses from his or her income, and capital gains are only taxed at half the amount of other income, the incentive still exists to buy the share. Generally speaking, it is unlikely that a donor will be willing to donate a flow-through share prior to receiving the deduction of expenses. However, regardless of whether the deductions are used by the donor, they are useless to the charity.

Flow-through shares are like any other asset and can be donated to charity. When these shares are publicly traded there is no tax on the capital gain (see below). However, for purposes of donation, the law considers the amount of the purchase price to be a capital gain and only the amount in excess of that (if there is any) to be eligible for the capital gains exemption.

Example:

Assuming the deductions from the shares are already used by the donor, imagine a situation where Elana bought publicly-traded flow-through shares for $5,000, and they are now worth $6,000. She can either sell them for $6,000 or donate them to a charity for $6,000. As the cost of these shares is deemed to be $0, if she *sells* them there will be a capital gain of $6000 (and a taxable capital gain of $3,000). At a tax rate of 46% she will have a tax liability of $1,380. So ignoring the value of the deduction, Elana must pay $1,380 of tax on a gain of $1,000.

On the other hand, when donated to charity, there is no tax on the increase in value greater than the purchase price. So, if these publicly traded shares are *donated* to charity, Elana will pay capital gains tax on the purchase price of $5,000 and receive a tax receipt for $6,000, which will offset approximately $2,760 of taxes including $1,150 from this transaction ($5000 being the deemed capital gain, only half of which is taxable multiplied by a 46% tax rate).

Table 1: Tax and credits resulting from the sale or donation of various values of publicly-traded shares

Purchase price	FMV of donation	Tax payable	Tax value of tax receipt	Credits remaining to offset other taxes
$5,000	$4,000	$920	$1,840	$920
$5,000	$5,000	$1,150	$2,300	$1,150
$5,000	$6,000	$1,150	$2,760	$1,610

Of course, when working with a particular donor, it may be in the charity's interest to have the donor purchase flow-through shares with the intention of donating them after the deductions are taken. In these cases, the charity should consult with an accountant to calculate the value of the relevant deductions in the donor's province of residence.

STOCK OPTIONS

Most businesses are organized as corporations, with ownership of the corporation divided into shares. Shareholders are entitled to, among other things, a share of the profits of the corporation. Shares of many corporations can be bought and sold on stock exchanges around the world, the price based on a perception of the future value of the company. As an incentive to employees to help increase the value of the company, both private and public corporations may offer employees the right to purchase shares of the corporation at some future date for a lower price than they are traded at on the stock exchanges.

Generally, the price at which employees can purchase the shares (the "strike price") is a set price. Assuming the employee exercises the option at a point when the fair market value of the share (i.e. market price) is greater than the strike price, the employee will pay tax on the difference between them.

In the 2019 budget, the Trudeau government proposed a system of distinguishing between options granted in large, publicly-traded corporations, and (usually smaller) Canadian Controlled Public Corporations. At the time of writing, the exact rules concerning this distinction are still not settled. However, it seems that the tax benefits of donating stock purchased under option plans will be restricted to those granted by smaller corporations — in line with the policy reason for the announcements in the first place.

Assuming the shares are publicly listed, if the employee exercises the option to purchase and donates them to charity within 30 days (and in the same tax year), there will be no tax payable on the disposition, and the donor will receive a tax credit for the full amount of the donation. If, on the other hand, the donor donates the options themselves, he or she may not be entitled to a receipt until the charity exercises the option — if ever. Given that this is, at the time of writing, an unsettled area of law, anyone interested in donating stock of any corporation acquired under an option plan should speak with an advisor with expertise in this area. For more background information, see the section earlier in this chapter on the donation of publicly-traded securities.

DERIVATIVES

While shares of publicly-traded corporations are the most popular form of security to be donated to charity, there are a variety of other sophisticated financial securities that may also be donated. Examples include: exchange-traded funds, index funds, hedge funds, warrants, rights, and put and call options. As long as these products qualify as publicly-traded securities, they will qualify for the special tax treatment accorded donations of this type.

PRIVATE SECURITIES

Despite the omnipresence of the CRA, Canada's income tax system is essentially self-administered. As a result, temptation abounds to conduct business with non-arm's length people (including oneself) in order to ensure a tax result that would not have occurred were all parties strangers to one another. Therefore, the ITA contains a variety of provisions designed to prevent taxpayers from surrendering to temptation.

One situation where a donor may be left in the position of too much control over a gift involves the donation of securities in a private corporation to a foundation controlled by the donor. The problem is easy to see; if one can donate securities of a corporation controlled by the donor to a charity controlled by the donor, the donor will be in a position to create a never-ending stream of tax receipts for donations of shares from which the foundation might not see any benefit.

Unfortunately, the ITA provisions to prevent this situation are drafted so broadly that they also affect donations to charities other than private foundations. Essentially, the donation of securities of private corporations is dealt with in one of two ways; either the gifts are "excepted," or they are not. An excepted gift is a share donated to a charitable organization or public foundation where the donor deals at arm's length with the charity, its directors/trustees, officers, and other like officials. Thus, a donor wishing to donate shares of a private company has an incentive to give them to a charity where he or she does not have any close relations serving in any capacity with the charity, and a disincentive to give them to a charity in which a close relation is serving in any capacity. In these latter circumstances, the gift is no longer an "excepted gift" and the rules for a "non-qualifying" security apply.

In cases where the gift has been donated to a private foundation or to a public charity to which the donor is related, the gift is not considered "made" until one of two things happen: either the item donated must cease to be a non-qualifying security (e.g. the corporation is no longer controlled by the donor, or the corporation becomes publicly listed), or the charity has disposed of the security within five years of receiving the donation. The fair market value of the gift is then the lesser of:

a) the value of the security when transferred to the charity, and

b) the value of the security when the gift is deemed to have been made.

Example:

Imagine that Naomi and Isaac own a very successful snack food business that they started from scratch. As a good community citizen, Isaac serves as a director of a public foundation in support of the local university. Seeing Isaac's commitment to this cause, Naomi wants to donate some of her shares in their business, worth $150,000, to the public foundation. If Naomi does this, the gift is not considered made until Isaac is either no longer involved with the foundation, or the foundation disposes of the shares (within five years of the gift having been made).

Let us further assume that three years later Isaac is still a director of the foundation and the business buys back the donated shares from the foundation for $100,000. Given that Naomi and Isaac started the business from scratch, to them the cost of the shares is likely negligible. They therefore have a capital gain in the year in which the charity sold the shares — the lesser of the value of the shares when donated ($150,000) and when sold ($100,000). (As these shares are not publicly-traded they do not qualify for the tax-free exemption discussed earlier). However, the taxation of these shares only occurs at half the rate it would have been if they had not been donated to a charity at all. Thus, of the $100,000, only 25% is taxable. On this $25,000, we apply our assumed tax rate of 46% to arrive at tax owing of $11,500. Naomi is still entitled to a tax receipt for $100,000, and would have tax credits totalling $46,000, more than offsetting the tax owing.

Note that the donor does not have to include any capital gain in their income before the shares are sold by the charity, so that the donor is not paying tax in advance of receiving the receipt. If the charity does not sell the shares within five years, the donor will not receive a receipt and the gain will never be taxable.

RRSPs/RRIFs

A *Registered Retirement Savings Plan* (RRSP) is a type of financial umbrella that allows deposits to accumulate tax-free until they are withdrawn from under the umbrella.

In the year in which money is contributed to an RRSP (i.e. put under the umbrella), it is deductible from the income of the contributor. Only certain types of assets can be deposited into an RRSP, but fortunately the list is quite long and includes cash, securities, and even gold bullion. Once in an RRSP, deposits can be converted from one form to another without any tax consequences. While the ITA allows income to accumulate in an RRSP tax-free, it does not allow an RRSP to exist forever. By the age of 71, one's RRSP must be converted into a *Registered Retirement Income Fund* (RRIF).

Money placed in an RRSP is not inaccessible to the owner of the RRSP; it can be withdrawn at any time but is taxable then. (Notably, there are exceptions for first-time home buyers and for those engaged in lifelong learning programs). Given the strong incentive to contribute to an RRSP, many Canadians involved in tax planning try to maximize their contributions, with the consequence that they do not have much income leftover to make large charitable contributions.

Nonetheless, people may find that they have more than enough money in their RRSPs once they get to a certain age and are willing to make donations in their lifetime in order to see the fruits of those donations while they are still alive. The RRSP rules do allow for withdrawals from the plan, but upon withdrawal the institution that holds the account (usually a bank) is required to withhold certain amounts. These amounts, on a per withdrawal basis (i.e. not cumulatively for the year), are:

- 10% (5% in Québec) on withdrawals up to $5,000

- 20% (10% in Québec) on withdrawals between $5,001 – $15,000

- 30% (15% in Québec) on withdrawals of more than $15,000.

The amounts withdrawn are claimed as income to the owner of the RRSP in the year withdrawn, and tax is paid at the owner's marginal rate. Thus, if a potential donor wants to donate $50,000 and has that money under the RRSP umbrella, a withdrawal of $50,000 would give the potential donor outside of Québec $35,000 cash to donate. The remaining thirty percent ($15,000 in this case) would be remitted to the government by the bank and credited as income tax already paid when the donor files his or her tax returns for that year.

A donor may also wish to donate his or her RRSP or RRIF upon death. There are two ways to do this. One way is to list the charity as a beneficiary of the RRSP in the donor's Will. The other way is to make use of the direct beneficiary election, which is signed when the RRSP is first opened (and can usually be changed at will). If the first method is used, the RRSP will fall into the donor's general estate before passing on to the charity. Under the second method, the RRSP will automatically become the property of the charity without going through the estate. The advantage of using the RRSP direct beneficiary election is that the RRSP will not pass through probate. When a Will is probated, the various provinces charge different amounts of tax on the total value of assets passed on in the Will. Thus, the amount of money in an RRSP is added to the other assets and a portion is taken by the government before any of the assets are passed on. In Ontario, these taxes are 0.5% on the first $50,000 of value in the estate and 1.5% on all amounts over $50,000.[13]

Also, probating a Will takes time and the charity might not be interested in waiting for that process to wind its way through the courts, particularly if the Will is being challenged by the other beneficiaries.

In the year of death, a taxpayer is entitled to offset one hundred percent of the tax owed by making donations. As one hundred percent of the RRSP income would otherwise be included as taxable income in the year of death, donating that amount to a charity would offset this income completely. It would also make use of the unlimited tax credit rule in the year of death.

INSURANCE

Anything that constitutes property can be transferred to another person. This includes contracts of insurance. For the most part, insurance has been overlooked by charities as a method of raising funds, but it is important for charities to be flexible in their thinking when sourcing donations. They may be able to amass donations of items they would otherwise never have sought, let alone receive. One such area that deserves further focus by charities is life insurance.

Life insurance is a product that is bought to plan for specific situations. In some cases, it is to provide for one's family at the death of an earner in a family, or to pay costs arising on death. However, life insurance also plays an important part in business arrangements, such as being collateral for a loan or providing funds for certain share purchase arrangements. No matter the reason that life insurance was purchased, it is always possible that the reason will cease to exist. For example, a business loan may have been repaid, or children in a family may have become financially independent. When the original reason for purchasing the policy disappears, the costs of the policy become unnecessary. By providing a place for the owners of superfluous policies to dispose of them, charities may realize significant revenue while playing a useful role in the economy.

From a tax perspective, the donor of a life insurance policy will have an income inclusion of the proceeds of disposition less the *adjusted cost base* (ACB). An income inclusion is distinct from a capital gain, and effectively means that a donation of an insurance policy has no net tax benefit for the donor. The ACB calculation is rather complicated and takes into account the premiums paid, dividends received, and (for policies purchased after 1982) the *Net Cost of Pure Insurance* (NCPI). Despite the ominous name, the NCPI is not overly difficult to calculate, although it will likely require professional advice from either an experienced advisor or the insurance company involved.

In a February 2008 bulletin, and later in another setting, the CRA laid down certain guidelines for determining the Fair Market Value of a disposed-of policy. In these

---

[13] This is not as big of an issue in every province and so it should be evaluated accordingly.

pronouncements, the calculation of the *proceeds of disposition* (POD) of an insurance policy takes into account:

- the policy's loan value;
- the face value of the policy;
- the state of health of the insured and his/her life expectancy;
- conversion privileges;
- other policy terms, such as term riders, double indemnity provisions; and
- replacement value.

The idea here is that the value of a policy may or may not be accurately reflected by any cash surrender value held by the policy. When valuing the policy for both tax and receipting purposes, the donor and the charity must take into account the fact that the donor may be very ill and the policy may mature shortly after donation. A policy that would otherwise be impossible to receipt would become valuable to the donor. To do this, the advice of an actuary and an appraiser is critical to correctly valuing the policy.

The charity may either cash the policy and use the funds immediately or pay the premiums on the policy and collect the larger death benefit when the insured dies. Of course, a very generous donor may not only donate the policy to the charity but also donate the yearly premiums to the charity. In this case, both the donation of the policy and the donated premiums would be receiptable.

ANNUITIES

An annuity is a contract under which one person deposits a sum of money with another in exchange for a subsequent income. It is basically the reverse concept of insurance. The income may be paid for either a specified period, for life, or for life with a minimum guaranteed period. Under the latter method, if the purchaser of the annuity dies during the guaranteed period, the annuity will be paid to some other person whom the purchaser had designated to receive it.

Although annuities are normally purchased from insurance companies or trust companies, life annuities are sometimes purchased from charities. Essentially, a person gives the charity a sum of money irrevocably in exchange for a promise by the charity to pay the donor a monthly income for life. The funds received would then be invested by the charity at a higher rate than it would pay to the donor.

Annuity payments are usually a blend of capital return and interest. Changes to the ITA result in different treatments for annuities made before and after December 21, 2002. For annuities issued before that date, only the interest portion is taxable. This interest may, however, be eligible for either the *interest income deduction* or the *pension income deduction* provided by the ITA. For annuities issued after December 21, 2002, the donor would be eligible to receive a receipt for an amount equal to the excess of the amount contributed by the donor over the amount that would be paid at that time to an arm's-length third party to acquire an annuity to fund the guaranteed payments.

Example:

If Daniel were to donate $100,000 to a charity and receive annual payments in return, and the charity purchased a $50,000 annuity to fund the payments, under the new rules Daniel would be entitled to a receipt for $50,000. If the annuity payments and the value of the receipt are greater than the amount actually donated, the excess will be included in income as the payments are received by the donor.

ARTWORK

The donation of artwork in Canada falls into two broad categories based on whether or not the artwork is certified *Canadian Cultural Property* and donated to a designated institution. Artwork that qualifies as *Canadian Cultural Property* is dealt with in the next section. Artwork which is *not* certified as *Canadian cultural property* qualifies as *Listed Personal Property* discussed later in this chapter.

CANADIAN CULTURAL PROPERTY

The Canadian government has set up the *Canadian Cultural Property Export Review Board* to certify which artwork or other item has cultural significance to Canadians. This does not apply only to works with a Canadian aspect, it applies to any cultural work that Canada may want to keep in its borders. If the donation is certified *and* made to a designated institution there is no tax due on the disposition. Thus, if the charity is hoping to attract donations of property with a particular cultural significance, it is important to secure the designation.

There are two categories of designation:

Category A is granted for an indefinite period of time to institutions that are well-established and meet all the criteria related to certain legal, curatorial and environmental requirements.

Category B is granted in relation to an institution involved in the proposed acquisition of an object (or collection) that does not meet all the criteria for designation, but which has demonstrated its capability to effectively preserve the type of property in question. More information on designation is available from the Department of Canadian Heritage on their website at: https://www.canada.ca/en/canadian-heritage/services/funding/movable-cultural-property/designated-organizations.html

The criteria by which the Board makes its decisions is beyond the scope of this book, but the Board has published a guide on the subject available here: https://www.canada.ca/content/dam/pch/documents/services/movable-cultural-property/certif-guide-eng.pdf

As a proper certification may involve many months of research, a request for certification should be made well before the donation is contemplated.

If a taxpayer donates certified property to a designated institution, there will not be any tax owing on the gift. In addition, the taxpayer is entitled to a tax receipt for 100% of the value of the gift (as determined by the Board).

Example:

Noa owns a first edition Captain Canada comic book that she purchased for $50,000. Noa, realizing that it might be of significant cultural value, asks the *Canadian Cultural Property Export Review Board* to assess the comic book. The Board does so and determines that the comic book is indeed of cultural value and that its fair market value is $100,000.

Noa then contacts the charity she has in mind, which happily agrees to accept the donation but confesses that they do not have "designated institution" status. In calculating her tax situation on donating the comic book, Noa does the following calculation:

Proceeds of disposition:	$100,000
Cost base	$50,000
Capital gain	$50,000
Taxes owing	$11,500
Tax credit	$46,000
Net taxes	$0
Leftover credit	$ 34,500

Realizing that she would have to pay $11,500 of tax on the gift, Noa contacts another charity, which does qualify as a designated institution. On this donation she would have no taxes and a leftover credit of $46,000. Clearly, Noa has an incentive to choose the designated charity. This incentive only increases in proportion to the value of the gift.

PROPERTY DONATED BY ARTIST

An artist who produces artwork for sale is considered to be producing inventory for a business. In this regard, the donation of artwork is considered a donation of inventory and treated as such (see below). Nevertheless, any artwork produced by an artist may qualify as Canadian cultural property regardless of whether it was produced for resale. When there is a gift or bequest of such cultural property, the rules described above with regard to such gifts will apply even though the property is not a capital asset.

INVENTORY

The determination of whether an item is inventory or capital is one of the most fundamental areas of our income tax system, but nevertheless is shrouded in vagueness and controversy. For example, to most people a house is a capital property, but if the owner of the home is engaged in the business of buying and selling homes the property becomes inventory of a business, and the question becomes, "When is one engaged in a business?" As discussed in Chapter 1, the distinction is important because while only 50% of the gain of capital property is taxable, 100% of the profit on inventory is taxable. Thus, in this context, there is a strong incentive for individuals to classify an item as capital instead of inventory. Nonetheless, the donation of inventory will result in tax credits that will at least offset the tax due on the disposition of the inventory.

> ### Example:
>
> Mia runs a business making stuffed animals. Her business is not incorporated, so all the income of the business is taxed at her personal rates during the year.
>
> After Mia has deducted all of her expenses, she is left with taxable income in the year of $50,000. If Mia sells one more toy that is worth $100, she will pay tax on that toy of $31. However, on donating the toy, she will be entitled to tax credits of approximately $40 (assuming that she has already made at least $200 of donations). Mia can then offset the tax owed by disposing of the last toy and using the additional $9 against the tax owing on her other $50,000 of income.

Of course, as income grows, so too does the tax rate, meaning that there are fewer leftover credits. In those provinces where the tax is equal to or greater than the credits generated by donation (which is all the provinces except Alberta) there would be no additional tax credits leftover for use. In Alberta, however, the credits will always more than offset the tax on the disposition of the donated item, even at the highest brackets.

Given the number of provinces, the multiplicity of tax rates and brackets, and the frequency with which they change, it is impossible to include a comprehensive chart showing the tax treatment of all donations of inventory in this book. An accountant should be retained to calculate the results of any donation of inventory.

PERSONAL USE PROPERTY

As we have seen, the ITA only allows for the receipting of property and creates several classifications for property each of which is accorded a different tax treatment. One such class is *Personal Use Property* (PUP), property that is owned by the taxpayer and that is primarily for the personal use and enjoyment of the taxpayer or persons related to the taxpayer. PUP includes:

- Bottles of wine
- Aeroplan points
- Air Miles
- Shoppers Optimum points
- Religious items
- Gift certificates
- Clothes
- Artwork
- Hobby items
- Comic books
- Model trains
- Toys
- Land (e.g. a fishing hole)
- Books

Normally, when these types of items are donated to a charity, the charity does not issue a receipt, nor does the owner expect one. This is, in most cases, the appropriate treatment. However, technically it does not have to be so.

The ITA specifies that for donations of PUP, the minimum cost is deemed to be $1,000. This is true regardless of the actual cost to the owner. The ITA also deems the item sold for a minimum of $1,000, again regardless of the actual sale/donation value.[14] So, when taken into the donor's tax return, there is no taxable event on items that are worth less than $1000.

On the other hand, a tax receipt can still be issued for these types of items. The value

---

[14] See Chapter 4 for more information regarding valuations.

on the receipt would reflect the item's *fair market value*. This receipt could then be used to generate some tax credits on the return (small though they may be). Charities should note, however, that valuing household items can be very difficult, and receipts should only be issued if value can be defensibly determined.

Example 1

Jonah bought a "Tickle Me Elmo" doll for $20. Shortly thereafter, it became a collector's item and the fair market value increased to $100. Realizing that there are needy children without a Tickle Me Elmo, Jonah donates the toy to a local charity. In return, he receives a tax receipt for the value of $100. On his tax return he calculates his capital gain as follows:

Deemed proceeds of disposition	$1,000
Deemed cost	-$1,000
Capital gain	0

As there is no capital gain, there is no tax payable. On the other hand, Jonah will receive a tax receipt for the fair market value of the doll ($100). Applying our assumptions (i.e. a tax rate of 46% and Jonah has already made at least $200 of donations), the $100 receipt will allow Jonah to claim back $46 of taxes owing from other sources.

The implication of this policy is that when items are donated which have an actual value greater than $1,000 but a cost lower than $1,000, the value of the donation will be enhanced because the amount of the capital gain will be reduced.

Example 2

Elliot decides to donate a model train set which he purchased for $100, but has it appraised in advance and discovers to his delight that it is actually worth $2,000. Elliot still decides to donate the train set to a willing charity, which issues him a receipt for $2,000. He then calculates his taxes as follows:

Actual proceeds of disposition	$2,000
Deemed cost	$1,000
Capital gain	$1,000
Tax	$230
Tax credits	$920
Total leftover credits	$690

There are three notes to make about the type of property donated.

First, make sure that the property is actually transferable. While premium points are property, some plans will not allow you to transfer the points to anyone else, and so they effectively cannot be donated. In this scenario, a donor may consider redeeming the points and then donating the actual item. Of course, this may prove to be of limited assistance to a charity that all of a sudden finds itself obligated to use a plane ticket to some place it did not want to go, on a date it did not want to travel.

Second, both the individual and the charity must obtain a reliable valuation. From the perspective of the individual, an improper valuation could lead to a donation tax credit disallowed by the CRA. The charity, on the other hand, has an obligation to issue proper receipts, so if the receipts are overvalued the charity may find itself facing uncomfortable questions from the CRA.

Finally, there are rules in the ITA which prevent situations where donors are buying and donating items that fall below the $1,000 threshold simply to create tax receipts to shelter income from other sources. While the charity will not necessarily be punished if involved in such a scenario, the donor could have the receipts disallowed.

LISTED PERSONAL PROPERTY

Listed personal property (LPP) is a subclass of PUP. It consists of certain specific items which are held both as an investment and as hobby items. The list includes artwork, stamps, books, coins and sculptures. Unless it is *Certified Canadian Cultural Property* (see earlier in this chapter) LPP has the same tax treatment as PUP.

REAL ESTATE

Generally, the donation of most real estate will be treated like the donation of any other type of capital property. If the item is inventory the donor will be taxed on the full proceeds of disposition, and if the item is capital the donor will only pay tax on fifty percent of the proceeds of disposition. There are, however, two significant exceptions to this rule.

a) **Principal residence**

The first exception is the donation of a principal residence. Canadian residents are not taxed on the gain arising from the appreciation of their principal residence. So if a donor bought his home for $100,000 and sells (or donates) it when it is worth $1,000,000, no tax will be payable on the appreciation in value (assuming the home was the donor's principal residence for that entire time).

If the donor were to donate the home to a charity, not only would there be no tax consequences on the disposition, but also they would receive a tax receipt equal to the fair market value of the home at the time of the donation. This can be useful for individuals who wish to offset any income they may have in the year of the donation or in the five following years (or in the two preceding years in the case of a bequest). However, depending on the amount of income the individual has, they might not be able to use the full amount of the receipt. This is especially true given that most Canadians have the bulk of their accumulated wealth tied up in the value of their homes.

In some cases, it might make sense for the donor to leave their home to a charity in their Will. By doing this, they might be able to use the tax credits from the donation to offset the income from the deemed disposition of their other assets and carry back the credits to the previous year. In both the year of death and the year preceding death, the estate can use the tax credits to offset up to one hundred percent of the income. Given that the deemed disposition of assets (with the exception of the principal residence) usually results in a large income in the year of death, the donor might, in fact, be able to do some significant tax planning in this way.

b) **Environmental property**

The donation of environmental property has a treatment similar to that of *Certified Cultural Property*. The treatment applies where property is designated as ecologically sensitive land by the Minister of the Environment (or a person designated by the Minister) and donated to any of:

- The Federal or a Provincial Government
- A municipality in Canada
- A municipal or public body performing a function of government in Canada
- A registered charity that has a main purpose (in the opinion of that Minister) of conserving and protecting Canada's environmental heritage, and that is approved by that minister or that person in respect of the gift.

In any of these cases, there will be no taxable capital gain on the donation.

We have described the specific tax treatment of items donated where there is no tax on the capital gain of the item in the sections on public securities and certified cultural property. The only significant difference is that tax credits generated from a donation of this type may be carried forward for ten years. The entire value of the donation is available to offset tax owing from other sources at the highest rates.

Environmental charities may want to suggest to potential donors that the tax benefits of reclaiming the property for the environment (prior to donation) may outweigh the costs of bringing it to the Minister of the Environment's standards. In this way, donors will pay for the costs of converting the property into ecological property (if possible) and will benefit from the absence of tax on the donation.

RESIDUAL INTERESTS

Most people who are familiar with the donation of property to charity do not realize that the bundle of rights that comes with the ownership of property can be divided in different ways. One of the ways to do this is to divide ownership of the property during one's life (called a *life interest*) from ownership on the death of that person (called a *residual interest*).

This is different from a property owner who owns the property and on death uses a Will to dispose of it in a manner he or she sees fit, because the residual interest owner in that circumstance can change their mind as they still own the property. Once the residual interest is sold or given away, however, the property will belong to the owner of the residual interest when the owner of the life interest dies. Only the owner of the residual interest can make changes at that point. A donor might consider this course of action in situations where they want to enjoy the income or use of the property during their lifetime and yet donate the property to the charity during their lifetime as opposed to on their death.

The value of the residual interest is calculated using an estimated value of the underlying property at the expected death of the donor (in itself determined from actuarial mortality tables) using present value dollars. This amount will be the value listed on the charity's donation receipt. Determining the fair market value of a property at the expected death of the owner at some point in the future is a complicated mathematical task best left to a qualified actuary and appraiser.

From a tax perspective, when the owner divides the rights and donates the residual interest, the donor would generally incur a tax consequence. The tax owing will be a function of the cost of purchasing those rights and their estimated value at the time of their disposition. Generally speaking this income will be treated as a capital gain.

Example:

Yechiel buys a cottage at the age of 50 for $100,000. He decides he would like a charity to have the property on his death, but he would like to enjoy the cottage during his lifetime. More to the point, he would like to use the tax credits now and enjoy the satisfaction of having made the donation while living. Yechiel consults an appraiser and an actuary, who together predict that in Yechiel's expected year of death the property will be worth $250,000 in today's dollars. Yechiel then donates the residual interest in the property to the charity. This entitles the charity to ownership of the property on Yechiel's death. In return, Yechiel receives a tax receipt for $250,000 which he can use against his taxes owing in this year and in the five following years. Even better, Yechiel is entitled to the income stream from the property should he decide to rent out the cottage during his lifetime.

Generally, there will be tax on the disposition of the residual interest (unless the property is, for example, a principal residence or ecological property being donated to an ecological charity). The capital gain is calculated according to a specific formula and depends on the gain in value of the residual interest relative to the entire property.

So, if Yechiel owned the property for some time before donating the residual interest, the tax calculation can become quite complex as it involves not only an estimate of the value of the property at the expected date of disposition but also a relative assignment of the cost of the property to the residual interest according to a specific formula. In any case involving the donation of residual interests, it is best to consult an experienced professional.

While technically the charity may pay for the maintenance and upkeep of the property, this cost is typically absorbed by the donor. Nevertheless, this should be the subject of a comprehensive agreement between the donor and the charity. Furthermore, the charity may want to make a notation on the title deed of the property indicating that it owns the residual interest, but even if the property is real estate not every jurisdiction allows this.

CHARITABLE REMAINDER TRUST

A trust is a legal device which effectively accomplishes one or both of the following objectives:

1. It separates the ownership of property (the capital interest) from the right to receive income from the property (the income interest), and

2. It can separate the person who legally controls the property from those entitled to benefit from it.

A *Charitable Remainder Trust* (CRT) is similar to the donation of a residual interest in that it allows the donor to donate the capital of the trust now, but the charity does not receive it until some later point (such as on the death of the donor). A CRT is particularly useful in situations where it is difficult to record the division of interests on title (such as artwork). Despite its legal potency, creating a CRT is simply a matter of signing the appropriate legal documents.

When a donor creates a CRT, he or she disposes of the residual interest in the property to the trust and then donates the certain rights in the trust to the charity (the "capital interest"). It is important to note that the donation in this case occurs when the owner transfers the interest in the trust to the charity. Thus, if the underlying property is, for example, publicly traded securities, the gift of an interest in the trust will not attract the same favourable tax treatment as donating the securities would have; it is a donation of an interest in a trust, not of securities.

The special tax treatment assigned to different types of property outlined elsewhere in this chapter (i.e., ecological property, publicly traded securities or certified cultural property) likely makes them inappropriate candidates for this type of donation.

It is important not to create the trust with the charity as the beneficiary, because if the donor is not careful he or she will gift an interest in the trust with no property (and thus no value on the receipt), and any subsequent disposition to the trust will not be considered a gift by the CRA. The appropriate method is instead to create the trust with the donor holding both interests in the trust. The donor then contributes the assets to the trust, and finally donates the capital interest to the charity. Of course, the donor would retain the income interest for herself as long as is set out in the trust deed.

As the tax consequences are similar to those experienced with a gift of residual interest, they are not explored here.

GIFTS TO U.S. CHARITIES

Individuals who reside in Canada and commute to their employment or place of business in the United States are allowed to deduct donations made to U.S. charitable organizations on the same terms as donations made to Canadian organizations.

There are, however, a number of other important conditions which must be met. Firstly, the commuter must live near the American border during the whole of the taxation year. Secondly, his or her U.S. employment or business income must represent their chief source of income for that year. Thirdly, he or she must be able to demonstrate that the gift was made to a religious, charitable, scientific, literary or educational organization created or organized in or under the laws of the United States. Finally, he or she must be able to demonstrate that such a gift would be allowed as a deduction under the United States Internal Revenue Code. Where all those conditions are met, the donations in question are treated as donations made to a registered charity.

VOLUNTEER SERVICES

The ITA makes it very clear that only a gift to a charity is receiptable. As explained elsewhere, a gift includes property or a right to property. Unfortunately, services do not qualify as property and, therefore are not receiptable.

This affects many different aspects of running a charity. For example, a painter who volunteers his services to paint the wall of a church cannot receive a receipt for the time he spent doing the painting. He can be reimbursed for the costs of his supplies but, of course, this is a separate matter. If, for some reason, the volunteer requires a receipt, the appropriate thing to do is to have an exchange of cheques for the services and the donation. So, in our example, the painter would invoice the charity for the amount of his or her work and the charity would pay the individual for the work. The painter would then turn around and write a separate cheque to the charity in the amount of the donation to the charity. In this way, the painter will have to claim as income the amount of the invoice and will get an offsetting deduction for the donation.

LOAN BACKS

In the context of donations there are really only two types of loan arrangements which involve charities. The first involves the donation of a gift and then the loan back of funds to the donor or someone who is non arm's-length to the donor. In these cases, the value of the receipt may be reduced by the amount of the benefit returned to the donor.

The other area in which loans involving charities occur involves the loan of capital items, generally artwork, from a donor to a charity. In these cases, donors often have a particular item of interest and want to enjoy it for their lifetime. For example, the owner may be prepared to donate the item to charity but wish to display the item in their home for as long as they live. Assuming the donor does not use a Charitable Remainder Trust to do this, they would donate the item to a charity, receive a receipt based on the fair market value of the donation, and the receipt would be reduced by the value of the loan back to the shareholder. It is important for charities to know that these types of arrangements are possible, but note that the valuation calculation is a complicated task best left to experienced professionals.

7 | Revenue and Receipting

Many people confuse the term charity with the term not-for-profit. Technically, these are different types of organizations. A not-for-profit, as the name would imply, cannot organize its affairs in order to earn a profit. A charity on the other hand *can* earn profit and generally engage in business relationships outside of simply obtaining donations. Examples of such activities include gift shops in hospitals and churches, charity bake sales and even rental income of property owned by charities. However, because charities are not taxable, Parliament has legislated limits to their involvement in the business world to ensure that they do not take advantage of this status to create an unlevel playing field with taxable businesses.

Charities also raise funds in other ways, and due to their charitable status these methods often involve the issuance of a charitable donation tax receipt. In order, however, to maintain the integrity of the charitable donation tax credit mechanism, the law contains a series of complicated provisions that apply in various situations. This is clearly necessary as every donation tax receipt issued involves foregone tax revenue on the part of the government, and it is important to ensure that receipts are only issued for gifts to charity. This chapter will review the rules regarding the different types of revenue a charity may receive, and outline some of the most common concerns regarding the issue of proper receipts.

BUSINESS REVENUE

There are concerns about allowing a non-taxable entity to compete without restrictions against for-profit corporations. This is not a trifling matter, as for-profit organizations are the backbone of our economy. On the other hand, it would be unfairly capricious to deny a charity the ability to earn revenue off of its assets — particularly as the income is generally used to support charitable activities. In fact, there is significant revenue to be gained from involvement in the business world that can be put to good use in a charity, but it comes with an accompanying concern regarding the risk to which charitable assets are exposed in the business world.

Charities are restricted from carrying out business that is unrelated to their charitable purposes where that business is not substantially run by people *not* employed by the charity. As a result, the first exception to running a business is one that is primarily run by volunteers. As most people that are involved in running a business are, by definition, paid employees, the exception for businesses run by volunteers is effectively limited to small operations of organizations with large volunteer bases.

On the other hand, a charity *may* run a business that is related to the charity's purposes and subordinate to that purpose. The first question that must be answered is whether or not the activity is in fact a business. For many organizations this determination will become necessary in separating a fundraising activity (e.g. a monthly bake sale) from a business activity (e.g. running a gift shop). Most of the guidance on the application of these rules is administrative (as opposed to statutory or common law), and a copy of the CRA guidance on this topic is available at **www.runningacharity.ca**.

Not all commercial activity is necessarily a business. For example, there is a distinction between a bake sale and running a bakery. A business is a commercial activity deriving revenue from the sale of goods or services undertaken with the intention to profit from this activity. There are certain indicators which may be found in running a business. They are:

a) Intention: the purpose of the activity is intended to generate a profit.

b) The *potential* to show profit: just because a business is unsuccessful does not mean that the operators did not have the intention and the ability to make a profit at some point. On the other hand, if the endeavour is structured so that it could never earn a profit then presumably it is not a business.

c) History of profit: just because an activity has fallen onto hard times, does not mean that the history of earning profit would be ignored.

d) The expertise of the people undertaking the activity: if the people who run the activity have experience and a history of running such for-profit activities, that would be an indicator that this may also be intended to be a commercial endeavour.

Soliciting donations is not going to qualify as a commercial business, nor does selling donated goods necessarily qualify. And the fact that fees are charged for the provision of certain charitable programs does not necessarily mean that the program will constitute a business. For example, neither rent for low-income housing, nor university tuition would qualify as a business if provided in the context of the pursuit of charitable purposes. However, the CRA does have certain economic development policies that should be consulted if the organization intends to engage in such activities as micro finance or employment of the hard-to-employ.

Another important issue is the frequency with which the activity is carried on. For example, a charity may decide to engage in an auction of donated equipment. Conducting such an event once is unlikely to attract the CRA's attention. However, doing so on a regular basis would (assuming the other criteria are also present) be a cause for some concern. The law in this area, however, is not entirely clear, and there is no bright line test to suggest how much activity is too much. From a policy perspective, conducting an activity once would likely not create the same level of concern with respect to competition with for-profit entities as conducting the activity on a regular basis. As the line between fundraising events and business becomes more distinct, the charity will run a greater risk of attracting unwanted CRA attention.

A. Related to charitable purposes

The issue of a link between the organization's charitable purposes and the business being proposed is critical but just because the income generated from a business activity is applied to an organization's charitable purposes is insufficient to form a link. The activity itself must be linked to the charitable purposes of the organization. The CRA has identified four forms of connection, and if the business falls into one of these categories it will be considered to be a business that is linked to the charitable purpose.

The first requirement is that the activity is a usual and necessary component of charitable programs. Put another way, these activities are generally necessary in order to conduct the charity's operations. For example, a hospital that has a parking lot, cafeteria or gift shop for use of patrons of the hospital. University bookstores and school uniform shops are also all considered necessary programs to improve the quality of the service delivered by the charity.

The second type of connection is activities that are an off-shoot of a charitable program. In these cases, the operation of the charity creates marketable goods as an off-shoot but not necessarily as the core programming of the organization. For example, an organization that intends to teach developmentally disabled adults life skills may produce artwork for sale; or an agricultural exhibit may produce flour or fruits and vegetables which could be available for sale.

Third, the charity may have excess capacity as a result of the general operation of its core programming. Clearly charities require physical space and staff in order to operate, and at times they may have excess capacity that they cannot use for any purpose. In these circumstances the charity would be well within its rights to rent out some of this capacity. For example, a charity may, in order to meet municipal regulations, be required to add residential accommodations to its premises. Unless the charity provides low-income housing, this is excess capacity which can be rented out to members of the public (one would have to be careful of the undue benefit rules). Another example may include a church that once had a Sunday school program which is now discontinued. That space could now be rented to some other school in full compliance with the law.

Fourth, the sale of items that promote the charity is clearly linked with the organization's charitable purposes. For example, Mothers Against Drunk Driving may create bumper stickers intended to remind people not to drink and drive. The sale of these bumper stickers would be linked to MADD's objects.

B. Subordinate

In addition to being related to the organization's charitable purposes, the business must be subordinate to the charity's real mission of undertaking good works. In other words, just because the activities are linked does not mean they can overtake a charity's general operations and remain compliant with the law. Unfortunately, this test is somewhat subjective, but if one is faced with a CRA audit it will be important to be able to show that the resources used in the business (including volunteer time) are a relatively small part of the charity's overall work.

The CRA has four indicators it uses to determine whether or not an activity is subordinate to the charity's main purpose.

First, a subjective analysis of whether or not the business activity is a minor portion of the charity's attention and resources. The difficulty in applying this test is apparent with respect to a volunteer's time. How is that to be determined as a measure of the resources available to the charity? Nonetheless, the CRA may look at the amount of time spent at board meetings discussing these issues or the allocation of an employee's time in managing a business. In certain circumstances where the endeavour is taking up an unusual amount of time, this may be related to a temporary circumstance (such as a bumper crop, or unexpected business opportunity) which should be brought to the CRA's attention.

Second, the CRA will look to see whether or not the business is integrated into the charity's operations or if it is acting as a self-contained unit. (This question may be related to that involving excess capacity). Obviously, if the business is a self-contained operation it is likely unrelated to the organization's charitable purpose, but even if it is related, it may not be subordinate to the organization's activities.

Third, an analysis as to whether the organization's charitable goals continue to dominate its decision-making. Over time all organizations are subject to mission creep, (the phenomenon where new activities tend to dominate the agenda of the group). It is crucial, whenever the organization does engage in some business activity, to always remember that it is a charitable organization dedicated to pursuing its charitable purposes.

Finally, the organization must be certain to continue to pursue its charitable purposes and allow no element of private benefit to enter its operations. While technically not an issue of subordination, it may be cause for revocation of the charitable registration if, for example, the organization provides unreasonably high salaries or employs more people than necessary to conduct its business.

Sometimes, the CRA latches onto business-related issues because they are anomalous in the charity's overall operation. Generally, this can happen where the charity is forced into a situation it did not foresee. In our practice we encountered an interesting example of this situation where, in order to comply with municipal law, a charity was required to provide additional street parking in front of its building. Unfortunately, providing such spaces was impossible, so it acquired an additional building on the block to allow it to meet the municipal requirement. Then, left with a building for which it had no need, the charity proceeded to rent the building out, thus engaging in an activity which was not related to its objects (the subordinate issue was another matter altogether). This true story of a charity easily be caught up in related business issues by following the law (in this case municipal) makes it crucial for charities to be aware of the various pitfalls that await when engaging in different types of revenue-generating activities.

INVESTMENT INCOME

Many charities have endowments (sums of money invested as capital to create income to support the charity's operations), clearly the investment of such income is an allowable activity on the part of charities. However, charities need to be extremely careful in investing their funds, as the protection of charitable property is of prime concern for the law generally.

Directors of charities have a duty to act prudently with respect to the charity's assets, but this does not mean that the charity cannot lose money in an investment. Prudent investments can sometimes lose money and risky investments can make money. Nevertheless, decisions must be made so that charitable assets are invested after due consideration and diligent review. Most provinces have rules in place (within their respective Trustee Acts) regarding certain behaviors involved in investments. For example, Ontario has rules involving the delegation of decisions to investment counsel. Any organization with a sufficiently large endowment should speak to qualified legal counsel to determine what their legal responsibilities may be. This is particularly important, as directors can remain personally responsible for imprudent investments.

Investments can take a variety of forms, among them government bonds, corporate bonds, common shares, preferred shares, loans and mortgages. Generally speaking, most of these investments are treated in the same way: once made the capital of these investments become subject to the disbursement quota rules described elsewhere in this book. Also, as a general rule, these investments should aim to earn approximately 3.5% in return to satisfy the disbursement quota in the following year without eating into the capital of the endowment.

Investment in shares of the operating business may run into certain other restrictions. In particular, a private foundation would be limited from holding certain shares under the excess business holding rules. These rules would effectively require a less than 2% holding in such a business, but the excess business holding rules do not apply to public foundations or registered charities.

All charities need to be careful about accepting donations of *non-qualifying securities*[15]. These are generally shares or bonds of private corporations which by their very nature to be illiquid and hard to sell. As a result, the *Income Tax Act* contains certain rules regarding receipting by certain charities, and effectively do not allow a charity the ability to receipt such items unless they are sold within five years of their receipt. Rules surrounding non-qualifying securities (explained in greater detail elsewhere in this book) are complicated, and qualified counsel should be sought if the charity is approached for a donation of this type.

SPONSORSHIPS

Many charities attract sponsorships from corporate donors. To the extent that the corporate donors receive value for service, the contributions are not receiptable. This raises the difficulty of attaching a value to the service the donor receives. For example, how much is an ad in a charity's bulletin worth? Just because the charity charges $100 does not necessarily mean that it is really $100 worth of value.

A donor that is a corporation is in the same after-tax position regardless of whether it donates funds to a charity or it makes a business deduction. That is to say, a donation tax receipt is a deduction of the same amount as an equal business expense, so the CRA and most businesses are often flexible about valuation. If the donor paid $10,000 for an advertisement which could only be valued at $5,000, then technically a charitable donation tax receipt should be issued for the other $5,000. However, whether the business received a receipt for the full $10,000 or $5,000 and the other $5,000 was a business expense, it would have the same net tax effect. In valuing these advertisements (for example) the charity should consult with an accountant who may be able to provide specific advice in those circumstances.

PURCHASING FOR THE PURPOSE OF DONATING

Generally speaking, receipts reflect the full fair market value of the item being donated. (A discussion of the meaning of fair market value can be found later in this chapter.) However, certain rules exist for situations where the donor has purchased something for the express purpose of donating it to the charity under the terms of a gifting arrangement. A gifting arrangement is effectively a tax shelter arrangement where a donor is encouraged to buy at a low price and donate for a high valuation. In these circumstances, where the purchase was made less than three years before the day that the gift was made, or where the property was purchased less than ten years ago, (but it is reasonable to conclude that when it was acquired one of the main reasons for that acquisition was to donate to the charity) the charity must issue a receipt for the *lesser* of the fair market value of the property or the cost of the property to the donor.

---

[15] See Chapter 6 re: Private Securities.

While the charity does not have to undertake superhuman efforts to determine the date which the property was acquired, or the value at which it was acquired, it would be sensible to at least make basic inquiries of the donor, who has an obligation to disclose this information. There are certain exceptions to this rule, they include:

- Inventory
- Canadian real estate
- Shares of publicly-traded corporations
- Ecological property
- Canadian Cultural Property Export Review Board-certified property
- Certain other shares or property of a corporation that is acquired in exchange for property which would otherwise be exempt from the receipting rule.

SPLIT RECEIPTING

A charity must issue a receipt for the full fair market value of items donated to it. However, in circumstances where the donor receives some benefit in return for his or her donation, the charity must reduce the amount on the receipt by the value returned to the donor. The rules also include a benefit returned to anybody not at arm's length to the donor. For example, if a charity is hosting a banquet and sells seats for $250 but provides a meal for $50 and entertainment worth $25, the value of the receipt of $250 must be reduced by $75 being the value of the benefits returned to the donor.

Example:

Rita buys a ticket to a Gala for the Fort McMurray Children's Charity. The ticket costs $200 and returns $65 in value for the meal and the entertainment. Rita's niece Yvette attends in Rita's place. The benefit being returned to Yvette must be deducted from the value of the receipt even though Rita did not attend the function.

The difficulty that arises in this circumstance is valuing the benefit returned to the donor. This is particularly true as the amounts contemplated are often very small. Where the issue involves large benefits returned (such as might be the case in corporate sponsorships), a certified valuator can be retained. For small amounts, such as the value of entertainment at a charity banquet, issuing a valuation can be rather difficult. In these circumstances it is worthwhile to speak with an accountant about the proper criteria for making such a valuation and the same would be true of any circumstance in which the charity returns a benefit to the donor either directly or indirectly. The goal is to not only to properly issue a receipt but also show the CRA that the charity was diligent in obtaining a reasonable — and defensible — valuation.

WHAT GOES ON THE RECEIPT?

We often encounter specific questions about what goes on the receipt. The rules in this regard are clearly outlined below.

Every official receipt issued by a registered organization shall contain a statement that it is an official receipt for income tax purposes and shall show clearly in such a manner that it cannot readily be altered:

a) the name and address in Canada of the organization as recorded with the Minister;

b) the registration number assigned by the Minister to the organization;

c) the serial number of the receipt;

d) the place or locality where the receipt was issued;

e) where the gift is a cash gift, the date on which or the year during which the gift was received;

   e.1) where the gift is of property other than cash

   i) the date on which the gift was received,

   ii) a brief description of the property, and

   iii) the name and address of the appraiser of the property if an appraisal is done;

f) the date on which the receipt was issued;

g) the name and address of the donor including, in the case of an individual, the individual's first name and initial;

h) the amount that is

   i) the amount of a cash gift, or

   ii) if the gift is of property other than cash, the amount that is the fair market value of the property at the time that the gift is made;

      h.1) a description of the advantage, if any, in respect of the gift and the amount of that advantage;

      h.2) the eligible amount of the gift;

i) the signature, as provided in subsection (2) or (3), of a responsible individual who has been authorized by the organization to acknowledge gifts; and

j) the name and Internet website of the Canada Revenue Agency. (i.e. Canada Revenue Agency — Canada.ca/charities-giving)

A receipt can include more than this, and should the charity wish to use the issuance of a receipt for any additional purpose such as perhaps thanking the donor or soliciting future donations, statements of this type may be included. The charity should make sure to retain copies of all receipts and should a receipt be cancelled or reissued for any reason, the CRA would require that the following information be present on all reissued receipts:

- All the usual required information;
- The serial number of the original receipt; and
- A statement that this new receipt replaces the original receipt.

Copies of sample receipts are available on **www.runningacharity.ca**.

WHO GETS THE RECEIPT?

Charities are sometimes given a cheque from a donor corporation but asked to issue a receipt to an individual. *The charity should not participate in such arrangements.* Receipts should be issued in the name of the donor. This means that if the donor is a corporation the receipt should be issued to that corporation as evidenced by the name on the cheque. In cases where it is impossible to tell who the actual donor is, the charity should be able to rely on the (written) word of the person making the actual physical transfer. This would be the case in situations involving cash.

WHEN IS THE RECEIPT ISSUED?

The receipt can be issued as soon as the gift is made. This is true even where there may be a condition subsequent to the gift. However, if the charity wishes to delay the issuance of receipts it can do so. This may happen where the charity is expecting regular monthly donations and wants to issue one global receipt for all of them. CRA guidelines are that charities can issue receipts as late as the end of February for gifts received during the previous year. While there is no formal law on this point, most donors appreciate receiving receipts sooner rather than later.

REPLACING A RECEIPT

From time to time a charity will issue a receipt that is then misplaced or accidentally destroyed by the donor. In these cases, the charity can reissue a receipt so long as it contains all of the required information, the serial number of the original receipt (and the new receipt) and a statement that it replaces the original receipt.

The copy of the original receipt kept by the charity should be marked with a note that it has been cancelled. The same process can be followed if a charity issued a receipt with incorrect information.

RETURNING GIFTS

Sometimes charities face the prospect of returning a gift to a donor. There are two ways this may arise. The first is where the donor, or the donor's family, request that the gift be returned. In these circumstances, a charity should know that returning a gift to a donor may put the charity off-side the rules regarding transfers to non-qualified donees. In other words, the charity may not be able to return the gift to the donor even if it wants to do so.

In other circumstances, the charity may wish to return the gift to the donor because the donor has committed some sort of public act with which the charity does not want to be associated. This happened famously in the case of David Radler, a former associate of Conrad Black, who made a large donation to Queens University, in return for which Queens put Mr. Radler's name on a wing of its business school. The day after Mr. Radler pleaded guilty to fraud charges in the U.S. Queens decided that they could no longer, in good conscience, be associated with him and attempted to return the gift to him.

Provisions within the *Income Tax Act* allow for the CRA to go back and reassess an individual who obtained the benefit of a charitable receipt for a gift which is then later returned. However, the obligation to not bestow a benefit on a non-qualified donee continues to exist. Thus, the situations in which a charity may be able to return a gift to a donor are typically those where there is a lasting condition attached to the gift which eventually allows the charity to return the gift if the condition is not met.

These conditions are rare as charities do not usually contemplate the return of a gift to the donor. However, if the charity is going to remain associated with the donor or the donor's family for a long period of time, it may be wise to contemplate such a clause at the time of the gift so that an option exists into the future.

8 | CRA Interaction

Given that the regulation of charities lies predominantly in the *Federal Income Tax Act*, it seems at first glance odd that regulation of the sector is inherently a provincial responsibility and not a federal one. That this is so, is primarily a matter of history (and the almost complete abdication by the provinces of their responsibilities). However, as regulation of the sector does fall to the CRA, the dispute resolution process tends to follow the same general framework as that for private taxpayers. This also extends to the filing of an annual information return similar to a tax return: the use of terms defined in the *Income Tax Act* are generally for other purposes but are also applicable to the regulation of charities and the calculation of monetary penalties.

The CRA's main mandate is to protect the integrity of the income tax base. Charities, by virtue of the donation tax credit, detract from that base, so there is an inherent conflict within the CRA between these two duties. This is not to say that the CRA has any incentive to revoke the registration of charities in order that its other mandate may be met, but rather that the people who enforce the law through the CRA are generally trained for the primary mandate rather than this secondary one.

This chapter attempts to describe some of the various issues which may arise in interacting with the CRA as a charity attempts to meet its responsibilities under the *Income Tax Act*.

T3010

The annual information return to be filed by charities within six months of their year-end is called the registered charity information return. It is form T3010 available on the CRA website or **www.runningacharity.ca** and is now filed online through the CRA CHAMP system described in Chapter 4

The T3010 document is designed for a CRA official to review and spot any obvious inconsistencies with the law. Of course, given the number of charities and the volume of information reported on the T3010, the Charities Directorate, lacking the person power needed to review these documents in anything but the most cursory way, only does so in any meaningful way prior to an audit.

Once it is received by the Charities Directorate, an officer will review the document to be sure that it is completed correctly and fully. The information in the document is then posted online, with the exception of certain confidential information such as the addresses of the directors. Making the information in the T3010 available to the public can pose certain public relations problems for charities, generally related to examination of their administrative expenses relative to the charitable expenses of the organization. Confusion about these expenses is compounded by the fact that the T3010 does not request standardized financial information but rather information that is of use in fulfilling the CRA's goal to determine whether or not the organization is in compliance with the law. For example, a typical income statement and balance sheet is not posted with the T3010.

Moreover, much of the information reported on the T3010 contains a subjective legal element — such as reporting of the organization's involvement in political activity — requiring the charity to make a legal determination regarding the characterization of the activity. And for the general reader, understanding non-standardized information with a legal judgment element — especially where the reader *does not know there is a subjective judgment* in the mix — almost inevitably results in confusion.

There has been some significant criticism and even a number of public relations problems caused by information (some of it even accurately filed) little understood by the reader. It is therefore critical that when filing their T3010, charities try to file the information with an eye towards what a third-party would understand when reading the information. For this reason, it is often useful to engage the services of an accountant or other financial professional who has experience in standardized reporting.

The T3010 document itself asks a number of rather specific questions that move from an identification of the charity and the people that run it to a brief description of its programs and finally a detailed list of questions on its financial transactions. The CRA publishes a guide to completing the T3010 document, called the T0433, which explains in detail each step required to complete both the document and its numerous schedules.

The structure of the T3010 and its subjective nature prevents us from providing a step-by-step description of its completion. Firstly, however, remember that it is a public document, and much of the charity's reputation for prudent spending could evaporate upon a reading of it, correct or incorrect, by the public. Take this document extremely seriously and direct specific questions to a professional charity advisor. Secondly, charities must file a full and complete return within the time frame allocated. A charity that files an inaccurate return is subject to revocation, and a charity which files a document beyond the time limit for doing so may be automatically revoked for failure to file. Therefore, charities should begin the process of completing the return as soon as possible after their year-end to give them time to complete it fully and submit it on time. Generally, this will also involve accurate bookkeeping throughout the year to make the filing as quick and painless as possible.

Providing information

There are two circumstances in which the charity may be asked to provide its financial information to the CRA. The first and most obvious involves submission of the annual return. The second is an audit of the charity itself. When a charity is being audited, it must provide the information requested. Refusal to do so is an offence in and of itself and can also lead to the revocation of the charity's status under an accusation by the CRA that the charity has simply failed to maintain adequate books and records.

In an audit situation, the charity must provide all information requested by the CRA. Exceptions exist for items which may be subject to privilege. This is usually solicitor/client privilege concerning communications with a lawyer, but certain other forms of privilege also exist. If a charity is going to claim that certain documents are privileged and will not be released to the CRA, it should consult a lawyer both to ensure that the claim of privilege is valid and about the proper methods in ensuring that privilege is maintained.

From time to time, the information contained in the charity's financial records may be of interest to the CRA in an investigation of other parties (generally donors). In these circumstances, the CRA may issue a *demand for information* regarding a particular donor(s) from a charity's files. The courts have generally held that the CRA has wide-ranging powers to request and receive information from a charity. This is not to say that a simple letter requesting information from the CRA must necessarily be obeyed. There are legal steps by which the CRA can formally and legally request documents of the organization. Depending on the nature of the request, it may indeed have the force of law and the charity may be compelled to reply. Again, legal counsel must be consulted to determine the charity's obligation to comply.

The release of information which may harm the financial interests of donors is, of course, a difficult decision for a charity. It is perhaps even more difficult when the release of the information may result in penalties against the directors of the charity themselves. Thus, a charity which receives a request for information from the CRA may properly ask that the request be formally made. This allows the charity to plausibly claim that it had no choice but to release the information.

DIRECTOR PENALTIES

In addition to the penalties described in Table 1, directors of charities, the charity itself, the individual signing receipts, and any individual aware of a receipt issued with certain improprieties can become liable to a penalty under the *Income Tax Act*. The penalty is 50% of the amount of the understated tax by the individual who could use the receipt. Generally, we assume that to be the amount of the receipt multiplied by the highest marginal tax rate in the province (see Chapter 1) multiplied again by 50%.

POTENTIAL PENALTIES

The *Income Tax Act* allows for charities to be revoked for even the smallest of transgressions. Realizing that this may be somewhat draconian, several years ago Parliament implemented a series of potential intermediate sanctions within the *Income Tax Act*. The sanctions range from a variety of monetary penalties to suspension, annulment or revocation of a charity's status, and a chart of these penalties is provided in Table 1. The CRA may also impose a compliance agreement, which is described in fuller detail below.

Table 1: List of charity penalties[16]

Infraction	Penalty/suspension for *first infraction*	Penalty/suspension for *repeat infractions*
Not filing an annual information return (Form T3010) on time	$500 penalty (assessed when an application for re-registration is made)	$500 penalty (assessed when an application for re-registration is made)
Issuing receipts with incomplete information	5% penalty on the eligible amount stated on the receipt	10% penalty on the eligible amount stated on the receipt
Not keeping proper books and records or not providing them to authorized CRA officials when requested	Suspension of tax-receipting privileges	Suspension of tax-receipting privileges
Charitable organization or public foundation carrying on an unrelated business	5% penalty on gross unrelated business revenue earned in a fiscal period	100% penalty on gross unrelated business revenue earned in a fiscal period and suspension of tax-receipting privileges
Private foundation carrying on a business	5% penalty on gross business revenue earned in a fiscal period	100% penalty on gross business revenue earned in a fiscal period and suspension of tax-receipting privileges
Foundation acquiring control of a corporation	5% penalty on dividends paid to the charity by the corporation	100% penalty on dividends paid to the charity by the corporation

[16] Source: http://www.cra-arc.gc.ca/chrts-gvng/chrts/plcy/csp/pnlts-eng.html

Infraction	Penalty/suspension for *first infraction*	Penalty/suspension for *repeat infractions*
Undue benefit provided by a charity to any person or entity (for example, a charity provides an interest-free loan to a director or non-qualified donee)	105% penalty on the amount of undue benefit	110% penalty on the amount of undue benefit. If the undue benefit is not conferred from a gift the suspension of tax-receipting privileges is also applicable.
Issuing receipts when there is no gift or when the receipt contains false information (when the total penalties **do not exceed** $25,000)	125% penalty on the eligible amount stated on the receipt	125% penalty on the eligible amount stated on the receipt
Issuing receipts when there is no gift or when the receipt contains false information (when the total penalties **exceed** $25,000)	125% penalty on the eligible amount stated on the receipt and suspension of tax-receipting privileges	125% penalty on the eligible amount stated on the receipt and suspension of tax-receipting privileges
Entering into a transaction, including making a gift to another registered charity, to delay expenditures on charitable activities	For the charities involved, a 110% penalty on the amount of the expenditure avoided or delayed	For the charities involved, a 110% penalty on the amount of the expenditure avoided or delayed
Accepting gifts or transfers of property on behalf of a suspended qualified donee	Suspension of tax-receipting privileges	Suspension of tax-receipting privileges
Private foundation not divesting itself of a percentage of its shares at the end of its fiscal period, in respect of a class of shares	5% of the result of multiplying the divestment obligation percentage of the private foundation for the fiscal period by the fair market value of all issued and outstanding shares in that class, except when there is a repeat infraction or another penalty for not disclosing, as indicated below, that applies for the fiscal period	10% of the result of multiplying the divestment obligation percentage of the private foundation for the fiscal period by the fair market value of all issued and outstanding shares in that class at the end of the fiscal period

Infraction	Penalty/suspension for *first infraction*	Penalty/suspension for *repeat infractions*
Private foundation not disclosing a material transaction in a class of shares at the end of its fiscal period when disclosure is required	10% of the result of multiplying the divestment obligation percentage of the private foundation in that class of shares by the fair market value of all issued and outstanding shares in that class for the fiscal period	10% of the result of multiplying the divestment obligation percentage of the private foundation in that class of shares by the fair market value of all issued and outstanding shares in that class for the fiscal period
Private foundation not disclosing a material interest held at the end of its fiscal period, by a relevant person, in a class of shares when disclosure is required	10% of the result of multiplying the divestment obligation percentage of the private foundation in that class of shares by the fair market value of all issued and outstanding shares in that class for the fiscal period	10% of the result of multiplying the divestment obligation percentage of the private foundation in that class of shares by the fair market value of all issued and outstanding shares in that class for the fiscal period
Private foundation not disclosing its total corporate holdings percentage at the end of its fiscal period in a class of shares when disclosure is required	10% of the result of multiplying the divestment obligation percentage of the private foundation in that class of shares by the fair market value of all issued and outstanding shares in that class for the fiscal period	10% of the result of multiplying the divestment obligation percentage of the private foundation in that class of shares by the fair market value of all issued and outstanding shares in that class for the fiscal period
Gifts other than *designated gifts* received from a non-arm's length charity that are not spent by the recipient charity on its own charitable activities or transferred to an arm's length qualified donee in the current or following tax year — this amount is in addition to a charity's *disbursement quota*	For the recipient charity, a penalty of 110% of the amount not expended or gifted	For the recipient charity, a penalty of 110% of the amount not expended or gifted

Infraction	Penalty/suspension for *first infraction*	Penalty/suspension for *repeat infractions*
Carrying out partisan political activities, or political activities that are not connected and subordinate to the charity's charitable purposes or carrying on political activities when the charity is not devoting substantially all its resources to charitable activities and purposes	One-year suspension of tax-receipting privileges	One-year suspension of tax-receipting privileges
Providing incomplete or inaccurate information on the annual information return (Form T3010)	Suspension of tax-receipting privileges until the required information is provided to the CRA on Form T3010	Suspension of tax-receipting privileges until the required information is provided to the CRA on Form T3010

The range of sanctions up to and including suspension are considered intermediate sanctions. However, despite Parliament's intention to give the CRA additional tools, the CRA effectively restricts itself to compliance agreements and revocation and very few intermediate sanctions have been levied since they were initially legislated in 2001. Thus, for charities facing potential sanction, the best case scenario would be a compliance agreement. The worst case scenario is generally revocation. It is therefore important to understand the circumstances by which the Charities Directorate decides to implement one punishment over another as described below.

CRA auditors often discover tax compliance errors which do not really fall within the scope of a review of the organization's charitable activities. This generally involves the issuance of T4 forms and other employee issues. It is not uncommon for the Charities Directorate to raise revocation as a punishment for these types of offences even though specific penalties exist for these types of transgressions.

PENALTY GUIDELINES

Given the range of possible punishments and the Charities Directorate's unfortunate reluctance to use the intermediate sanction tools given to them by Parliament, the Directorate has developed a continuum by which it decides when the offence is so severe that it will pursue revocation rather than a compliance agreement — generally skipping the intermediate penalties. This document, *Guidelines for Applying Sanctions*, is available at **www.runningacharity.ca.**

First, the CRA analyzes the charity's non-compliance to determine the severity of the offence, and the criteria it considers will include whether the charity has been warned before, the amount of money at stake, whether the activity involved was a tax shelter/criminal/terrorist activity, and whether it can legitimately be said that the charity knew better.

Added to the concerns the Directorate lists in its guidelines are certain unstated matters. It will also make a subjective analysis of the type of organization facing revocation. Certain larger charitable organizations, while not untouchable, are of a type that their revocation would pose great difficulties for the Charities Directorate from a political perspective — for example, universities and hospitals. We are unsure how the Directorate makes this analysis, but it does seem clear that it will take a softer hand for certain organizations that may otherwise face revocation.

Depending on the Directorate's analysis of the appropriate punishment, it may levy one of a number of penalties. The most basic response to an audit is what the CRA calls an education letter. These letters are relatively rare, but effectively offer advice to the charity in terms of its compliance and ensuring that it remains onside of the rules. The next most severe punishments are compliance agreements (described in greater detail in the next section) that effectively force the charity to agree that it is not in compliance and will be in compliance in the future. If a later audit determines that the organization is still not in compliance, the Directorate may then decide to pursue revocation as the charity has been previously warned.

In theory, the CRA may decide to pursue an intermediate sanction that could include a financial penalty or suspension of the charity's status, but these penalties are effectively ignored by the Directorate. The final, and most serious, punishment is revocation. (Annulment of a charity is also a possibility but is only used where the charity was either improperly registered in the first place or the law has changed such that the charity no longer qualifies for registered status. We do not consider this an intermediate sanction, because it is not a punishment for something the charity has done wrong; rather it is a necessary mechanism to deal with changes in the law.)

COMPLIANCE AGREEMENTS

Charities are often left hoping for a compliance agreement as opposed to the more serious sanction of revocation but should be wary of signing them. Firstly, compliance agreements generally require the charity to admit fault, and this admission can, and will, be used against the charity in any future decision by the CRA to revoke the organization's status based on the same offence. Secondly, this admission of guilt could be used by the CRA as justification to assess the donors to the charity if the admission relates to their donations. We have seen situations where the charity signs a compliance agreement because it seems the best alternative, but then suffers public relations disasters because the CRA insists on assessing all the donors as a result. The charity is then in the unfortunate position of having to explain to its donors why it effectively told the CRA to reassess the donors.

Furthermore, just because the "punishment" being offered is not revocation does not necessarily mean that the Charities Directorate is correct in its position that the charity was offside the rules in the first place. We have seen other situations where the Directorate has proposed a compliance agreement for circumstances in which there is doubt that the charity (at least in its own mind) did anything wrong. Unfortunately, if the charity does not sign the compliance agreement, it is left to the CRA to decide whether or not to pursue revocation. Should the CRA pursue revocation, the charity is immediately forced into the appeal process described below. This process itself can be a punishment, given the cost and resources required for the charity to defend itself.

Charities are thus often in a difficult no-win position in deciding whether to sign the compliance agreement, thereby admitting fault but avoiding the difficulties of defending itself, and the additional public relations problems that result from admitting offence. Nonetheless, there is room to negotiate the terms of the agreement. The CRA will not change the substance of the agreement, but there may be room to negotiate the wording around the admission of guilt. Although such agreements are not supposed to become public, there are circumstances where they can, and changes to the wording can have important consequences. Under these circumstances, organizations considering a compliance agreement should consult with experienced legal counsel to determine whether it is appropriate to sign it and the consequences that may follow.

OBJECTIONS

If the CRA decides to proceed with revocation, the charity will receive a letter entitled *Notice of Intent to Revoke*. This begins the 'winding-up period' discussed elsewhere in this book. An organization that wishes to avoid revocation must file a *Notice of Objection* to the Charities Redress Section at this address:

Tax and Charities Appeals Directorate
Appeals Branch
Canada Revenue Agency
250 Albert Street
Ottawa, ON K1A 0L5

The same approach would be followed by a prospective charity that received a *Notice of Refusal to Register*. An organization that is revoked for failure to file the annual T3010 return would generally not choose to object but would rather file a new application for charity status along with the T3010 and a $500 filing penalty fee.

The Charities Redress Section is typically staffed with people who have some level of seniority and who understand the context and laws under which a charity operates. Their job is to ensure that the Charities Directorate has applied its mandate correctly, so a charity cannot necessarily expect that the case will have a different disposition at the Redress Section. Rather, the question will simply be whether the particular officer has properly applied the law. It may be that all the facts were not presented to the original officer, so this is an opportunity to further illuminate the file for the Redress Section officer (and sometimes in preparation for an inevitable court hearing). Another possibility may be that, based on a determination of the *Guideline for Intermediate Sanctions* the Directorate improperly revoked because the severity of the infraction was not of a type that should elicit revocation.

An appeal to the Redress Section should not be considered another 'kick at the can.' The Redress Section is a check of the actions of the Directorate, and only if there is room to argue that the decision was improperly made, can there be a hope for success at the Redress Section.

Once a *Notice of Intent to Revoke* is received, the charity has ninety days to file its *Notice of Objection*. The Redress Section is much smaller than the Directorate and currently seems unable to deal with the volume of objections in a timely fashion. A charity can expect a significant delay between filing a *Notice of Objection* and the time when an officer is assigned to the case. It is not unheard of for the delay to exceed one year. During this time, the organization is in the winding-up period described in Chapter 10.

The revocation process is not complete until the CRA publishes the final *Notice of Revocation* in the *Canada Gazette*. This revocation can be finalized as soon as thirty days after the *Notice of Intent to Revoke* is sent, but such quick action is typically reserved for organizations involved in tax shelters and what the CRA terms to be aggravated non-compliance.

The Court, on the other hand, applies a somewhat different test to determine whether immediate revocation is appropriate. That test involves an examination into the harm caused by an immediate revocation (rather than waiting for the charity's appeals regarding the CRA's reasons for revocation to be heard), and whether that harm can be remedied through the payment of money (although there are other parts of this test as well). Sometimes charities are in the frustrating position of having lost their charitable status while still waiting to hear from the Redress Section as to the merits and demerits of revocation. Unfortunately, the law allows such a situation, and a charity facing this may retain a lawyer to file the appropriate request for a stay at the Federal Court of Appeal.

If, after filing a *Notice of Objection*, the delay at the Charities Redress Section exceeds 90 days, the charity can skip the rest of the wait and file its *Notice of Appeal* at the Federal Court of Appeal. Of course, this means that if the charity had a viable case at the Redress Section it misses the opportunity to resolve the matter at that level and avoid the legal fees associated with an appeal to the courts.

As described in the Chapter 10 section on revocation tax, a revoked charity could become liable for what is known as the revocation tax. Under certain circumstances a charity may receive a *Notice of Assessment for Revocation Tax* from the CRA indicating that the (now revoked) charity owes some amount of revocation tax. If the organization wishes to object to the *Notice of Assessment* it will file a *Notice of Objection* to the revocation tax to the Charities Redress Section at the address already provided. The content of this notice would include, besides the name and address and business number of the charity, the actual circumstances for the proper calculation of the revocation tax. Under most circumstances, it will also include a filing of the T2046 if it was not done previously.

If there is a dispute over what is properly included in the revocation tax, an appeal from a decision of the Charities Redress Section in relation to the revocation tax will go to the Tax Court of Canada rather than the Federal Court of Appeal. In both cases, a knowledgeable tax litigation lawyer should be retained to resolve the matter.

APPEALS

Charities that receive an unfavorable result from their appeal to the Charities Redress Section may consider an appeal to the Federal Court of Appeal, or, for appeals of Revocation Tax, to the Tax Court of Canada. At the Federal Court of Appeal an incorporated entity must be represented by legal counsel. Appeals to the Federal Court of Appeal must be approached seriously and it would be unlikely that an organization could be successful without retaining qualified legal counsel immediately upon learning it must file to the court. The same is true of appeals to the Tax Court of Canada.

9 | Spending Money

In any country in which the government subsidizes donations, strict legislative restrictions are in place on the spending of those donations and Canada is no different. However, Parliament's efforts here are hindered by the fact that the constitutional power to regulate charities lies with the provinces. The Federal Government is (at least technically) restricted to legislation reasonably related to the implementation of an income tax. And one could argue — although it has not been done yet — that details of spending by charities would therefore be beyond the jurisdiction of the Federal Government. Nevertheless, the *Income Tax Act* contains a variety of provisions that effectively ignore this limitation, and that have been expanded upon over time by the CRA and the Courts. This chapter reviews those restrictions and provides an outline by which organizations can guide themselves when spending their charitable funds.

DISBURSEMENT QUOTA

Paragraph 149.1(1) of the *Income Tax Act* defines a charitable organization as:

> "...at any particular time, means an organization, whether or not incorporated, all the resources of which are devoted to charitable activities carried on by the organization itself ..."

On its face, this seems to mean that a charitable organization (i.e. not a foundation) can only use its assets and resources in pursuit of its charitable objects. While generally the law is to be read as simply as possible, in this case it was never understood to mean exactly as it seems. Instead, charities have always been allowed to pursue administrative activities necessary for their general operation, even if this seemingly violates the principle that they must devote *all* of their resources to the pursuit of their own charitable activities. This includes everything from fundraising to hiring staff and the use of professional advisors incidental to running a functioning organization.

When the law was originally drafted in the 1970s it was understood that there would need to be some sort of relieving provision to allow charities to spend some of their resources on non-charitable activities. This provision was originally intended to be the disbursement quota (DQ). The actual DQ formula began simply and evolved into a creature with five variables and various definitions unintelligible to practically everyone. Fortunately, the formula was simplified as follows:

> "Disbursement quota," for a taxation year of a registered charity, means the amount determined by the formula:
>
> **A × B × 0.035/365**
>
> where,
>
> A is the number of days in the taxation year,
>
> and B is
>
> (a) the prescribed amount for the year, in respect of all or a portion of a property owned by the charity at any time in the 24 months immediately preceding the taxation year that was not used directly in charitable activities or administration, if that amount is greater than
>
> (A) if the registered charity is a charitable organization, $100,000, and
>
> (B) in any other case, $25,000, and
>
> (C) in any other case, nil.
>
> Understanding this definition can be further simplified.
>
> Generally, variable "A" will be 365 (days). It would be shorter in a year in which the charity begins or terminates its operations (And in a leap year it is 366). Variable "B" refers to a "prescribed amount." The prescribed amount is defined in the Regulations to the *Income Tax Act* and can be easily changed by the bureaucracy (although this has not happened since the disbursement quota provisions were amended in the 2000's). The prescription for variable "B" is rather complicated but we have nevertheless reproduced it below.

Regulation 3701

1. For the purposes of the description of B in the definition "disbursement quota" in subsection 149.1(1) of the Act, the prescribed amount for a taxation year of a registered charity is determined as follows:

a) choose a number, not less than two and not more than eight, of equal and consecutive periods that total twenty-four months and that end immediately before the beginning of the year;

b) aggregate for each period chosen under paragraph (*a*) all amounts, each of which is the value, determined in accordance with section 3702, of a property, or a portion of a property, owned by the registered charity, and not used directly in charitable activities or administration, on the last day of the period;

c) aggregate all amounts, each of which is the aggregate of values determined for each period under paragraph (*b*); and

d) divide the aggregate amount determined under paragraph (*c*) by the number of periods chosen under paragraph (*a*).

2. For the purposes of subsection (1) and subject to subsection (3),

a) the number of periods chosen by a registered charity under paragraph (1)(*a*) shall, unless otherwise authorized by the Minister, be used for the taxation year and for all subsequent taxation years; and

b) a registered charity is deemed to have existed on the last day of each of the periods chosen by it.

3. The number of periods chosen under paragraph (1)(*a*) may be changed by the registered charity for its first taxation year commencing after 1986 and the new number shall, unless otherwise authorized by the Minister, be used for that taxation year and all subsequent taxation years.

Determination of value

Regulation 3702

1. For the purposes of subsection 3701(1), the value of a property, or a portion of a property, owned by a registered charity, and not used directly in charitable activities or administration, on the last day of a period is determined as of that day to be:

a) in the case of a non-qualified investment of a private foundation, the greater of its fair market value on that day and its cost amount to the private foundation;

b) subject to paragraph (*c*), in the case of property other than a non-qualified investment that is

i) a share of a corporation that is listed on a designated stock exchange, the closing price or the average of the bid and asked prices of that share on that day or, if there is no closing price or bid and asked prices on that day, on the last preceding day for which there was a closing price or bid and asked prices,

ii) a share of a corporation that is not listed on a designated stock exchange, the fair market value of that share on that day,

iii) an interest in real property or a real right in an immovable, the fair market value on that day of the interest or right less the amount of any debt of the registered charity incurred in respect of the acquisition of the interest or right and secured by the interest or right, where the debt bears a reasonable rate of interest,

iv) a contribution that is the subject of a pledge, nil,

v) an interest, or for civil law a right, in property where the registered charity does not have the present use or enjoyment of the interest or right, nil,

vi) a life insurance policy, other than an annuity contract, that has not matured, nil, and

vii) a property not described in any of subparagraphs (i) to (vi), the fair market value of the property on that day; and

c) in the case of any property described in paragraph (*b*) that is owned in connection with the charitable activities of the registered charity and is a share of a limited-dividend housing company referred to in paragraph 149(1)(*n*) of the Act or a loan, that has ceased to be used for charitable purposes and is being held pending disposition or for use in charitable activities, or that has been acquired for use in charitable activities, the lesser of the fair market value of the property on that day and an amount determined by the formula:

(A / 0.035) x (12 / B)

Where

A is the income earned on the property in the period, and
B is the number of months in the period.

2. For the purposes of subsection (1), a method that the Minister may accept for the determination of the fair market value of property or a portion thereof on the last day of a period is an independent appraisal made

a) in the case of property described in subparagraph (1)(*b*)(ii) or (iii), not more than three years before that day; and

b) in the case of property described in paragraph (1)(*a*), subparagraph (1)(*b*) (vii) or paragraph (1)(*c*), not more than one year before that day.

As the DQ, at this point, is intended to force charities to spend a percentage of their assets not used directly in charitable activities in the previous 24 months, it is important to assign a value to those assets which qualify. These provisions, as complicated as they are, effectively allow a charity to average out the value of those assets so that it can complete the calculation. Such averaging provisions are clearly required considering that the value of a stock portfolio is in constant flux. Once this averaging is completed, the application of the rest of the formula is relatively clear.

Assets not used in charitable activities are typically endowments (generally cash) that are invested so that the charity may benefit from the income earned on the amounts. At times, a charity may attract donations greater than that required for its operational use, so it forms the corpus of an investment portfolio for the future benefit of the organization. For example, an organization with an endowment of $100 000 in 2019 would be obligated to spend 3.5% of that amount in the year 2020. This means that the organization should aim to earn at least 3.5% on its principal so that it can meet its quota in 2020.

Organizations that transfer funds from themselves to another organization and then have spending done by the other organization do not benefit from a double dip in the amount of the disbursement quota. At least one of the organizations must spend the money on charitable activities. Nevertheless, there may be a one-year deferral, depending on the circumstances of the transfer.

There are a couple of important notes to make about the DQ. First, the DQ always acts one year in arrears. For example, the spending requirement in year two depends on the assets not used in charitable activity in year one. Second, with the exception of the minimum threshold levels, the disbursement quota affects private foundations, public foundations and charitable foundations in the same way. Third, charities that are planning to undertake large capital expenditures may be building up a large amount of capital in order to purchase something — for example, a building. If that is the case, the charity should contact the CRA to request an exemption for the calculation of the DQ. To do so, a letter with the following information should be sent to the address below or filed in the charity's My Business Account:

- the specific purpose for which the funds will be used

- the amount required

- the length of time needed to accumulate the funds (minimum 3 years and maximum 10 years)

- the signature of a director/trustee or other authorized representative of the charity

- the name and the registration number of the charity

- the effective date (starting date)

Mail or fax the letter to:
Charities Directorate
Canada Revenue Agency
Ottawa ON
K1A 0L5

Finally, sometimes, in circumstances beyond its control, the charity may be unable to meet its DQ. This may happen in cases of theft from the charity, or simply a dramatic financial downturn (such as happened in 2008). In these cases, the charity may ask the CRA to consider a DQ reduction. Such a reduction will only be considered if the charity has already applied any available DQ excess against the year from either previous or later years. To request a reduction, the charity must complete form T2094 (available on **www.runningacharity.ca**).

FUNDRAISING EXPENSES

The constitutional authority of the Federal Government in legislating regulations for charities is limited, and this is implicitly recognized in the document put out by the CRA documenting its expectations for fundraising. It is entitled *Fundraising by Registered Charities* available on **www.runningacharity.ca.**

The fact remains, however, that fundraising expense *is* an issue of tremendous concern to the public. Consequently, the CRA has assumed the role of regulator of charities in the public interest and has provided guidance on appropriate fundraising expenses. Even if there is no particular legal provision on which the CRA could rely to revoke a charity specifically for extraordinarily high fundraising expenses, there are many other provisions that the CRA could use to build a case for revocation, relying on the same facts.

The guidance defines "fundraising" as the solicitation of any type of donation. Clearly, charities cannot engage in deceptive or illegal activity to fund raise (although this is not an income tax rule). Neither can they make fundraising their primary activity. Some charities run into problems when they use third-party fundraisers that bill the charity for their services. In these cases, where the CRA finds the expenses paid objectionable, they will make the argument that the charity now exists to benefit these third parties rather than to pursue their own charitable objects. So, charities hiring third-party fundraisers should be careful about their arrangements.

Appropriate fundraising expenses are calculated as a percentage of revenue in the year. It is a fairly easy calculation, as all fundraising expenses (including appropriate allocations of staff time and office resources) are divided by the charity's total fundraising revenue in the year. Fundraising revenue includes both receipted and unreceipted donations but is not limited to revenue raised directly as a result of a specific fundraising activity. Effectively, calculating in this way averages out the fundraising expenses for a specific campaign over all of the revenue raised by all fundraising campaigns.

Clearly, this benefits organizations with large fundraising efforts, and allows them to spend a greater percentage of revenue on starting a specific campaign than would a smaller group. Recognizing this, the CRA tries to make allowances for charities with less than $100,000 in revenue.

Fundraising expenses are divided into three bands: 35% and under, 36% to 70% and over 70%. The first band of fundraising expenses is unlikely to raise concerns from the CRA.

The second band, however, would raise concerns at the CRA, and the charity would have to explain why its ratio is so high (of course the higher the ratio, the better the explanation would have to be). For example, in some circumstances an organization may be undertaking some sort of acquisition campaign to seek new donors and for a limited period of time may have rather high fundraising expenses. If that is the case, the CRA would look for decreasing expenses over time as the organization's revenue increases.

Fundraising expenses in excess of 70% of an organization's revenue will be considered inappropriate. Again, while the CRA cannot technically revoke for excessive fundraising expenses, one can confidently predict that the CRA will very likely find some other grounds on which to revoke such an organization — such as that it exists for the unstated and uncharitable purpose of fundraising. It should also be noted though that the CRA is not completely oblivious to the situations in which charities operate and is generally approachable when explaining extenuating circumstances that lead to higher than anticipated fundraising expenses.

Regardless of the CRA's position on fundraising expenses and its constitutional authority in that regard, the fact remains that the public is intensely interested in the administrative expenses of charities. Any charity with excessively high fundraising expenses is undertaking a risk.

DEALS WITH BOARD MEMBERS

As a rule, charities try to collect board members from different walks of life. This is generally so they can benefit from the varied experiences of those around the table. Periodically, directors have access to goods or services that the charity may require. This is often true of lawyers and accountants, but it is equally true of painters, electricians and businessmen.

Since the directors are typically in a position to know the charity's needs, they are tempted to provide their goods or services to the charity for a fee. These transactions are generally prohibited by common law, as directors have a duty not to benefit from the assets of the charity. This includes *any benefit* and not simply a duty not to be paid in their role as director. Thus, directors are generally forbidden from selling their goods or services to the charity *for any amount*.

If a charity and the director agree that they require this particular service from the director, the charity may get approval from a court to engage in this transaction. Only

Ontario has a procedure which makes such a request routine.[17] In other provinces, the courts may not even have any idea that they have this authority, and it is thus difficult to get such approvals. Under the common law, a director who benefits from a charity's property in this way could be forced to repay every penny they billed to the charity. (It is our understanding that this has never happened in Canada, but then again, nobody wants to be the first!)

From an income tax perspective, the CRA's jurisdiction extends only to situations where a director or member of the charity receives a benefit to which they were not due. This involves either a payment in excess of fair market value of goods and services provided, or where the charity foregoes receiving income to which it would be entitled, for the benefit of a director or member.

This provision effectively allows the CRA to punish the charity for bestowing the undue benefit, whereas the common law is intended to punish the director. This of course, assumes that the charity had the legal authority in the first place to engage in a business relationship with the director.

MAINTAINING CONTROL AND DIRECTION

The definition of a "charitable organization" is one where the organization conducts its own charitable activities. This implies that a charity is *restricted* to dedicating its resources to carrying out only its **own** charitable activities. Carrying out one's own charitable activities is understood to require the charity to maintain control and direction over its resources as those activities are conducted. Where the charity is actually the one conducting its activities, this is not a problem. For example, a charity whose volunteers are operating a soup kitchen will clearly have control over its resources. Similarly, an organization that sends volunteers to conduct operations abroad would appear to have control and direction over the resources being used to implement those activities.[18]

However, the situation becomes more difficult where a charity is working with a partner, for example, a 'Canadian friends of' organization that works to help people in a foreign jurisdiction. In this case, the organization may not actually send volunteers to implement the activities, but to do so may work with a group or organization in that country. Maintaining control and direction over the spending of funds is the fundamental requirement of an organization that is operating either locally or abroad. The test for control and direction does not apply simply to an organization's actual cash, but also to the goods purchased with those funds.

Control and direction means that decisions over the charity's resources are made by the charity itself. This must be the case whether the charity operates only in Canada or elsewhere as well. While applying the test may vary in different circumstances,

---

[17] See the Public Guardian and Trustee for more information.

[18] Obviously, transfers to other qualified donees are allowed.

the overall effect is the same, and charities must ask themselves whether they have outsourced the decision-making over their resources to others (unacceptable) or are listening to the advice of others and making their own decision (acceptable). Indicators to consider would include what would happen if the charity decided to pull out of the specific project. Could the charity receive back any goods or property it has purchased? Would it be able to identify which items it owns and which it doesn't? And could it determine that all of its resources to date have only been used to pursue its charitable purposes? These are all questions that CRA auditors will ask if brought in to review the situation.

Many Canadian charities operate overseas with foreign partners. Where the Canadian charity sends funds abroad, it must ensure that it maintains control and direction over those funds — and any property purchased with them. To make matters still more difficult, CRA auditors can only judge control and direction if proper documentation is kept.

When an auditor looks at a charity, he or she seeks to find evidence that the funds of the charity were never used for non-charitable purposes, and that they *could* never have been used without the charity's explicit authorization. The organization must show not only that the funds *could not* have been spent on non-charitable activities, but also that in fact they *were not* spent on non-charitable activities. The CRA recommends that when carrying out activities through an intermediary, the following steps are undertaken:

a) Create a written agreement with the intermediary and implement its terms.

b) Communicate a clear, complete and detailed description of the activity to the intermediary.

c) Monitor and supervise the activity.

d) Provide clear, complete and detailed instructions to the intermediary on an ongoing basis.

e) Arrange for the intermediary to keep the charity's funds separate from its own, and to keep separate books and records.

f) Make periodic transfers of resources, based on demonstrated performance.

The evidence a charity may use to prove it has control and direction over its resources will vary with the circumstances. Clearly, where a transfer of funds is involved it will necessitate banking documents, including a separate bank account and copies of foreign exchange receipts as well as any other financial documents showing the transfer of funds and the spending of those funds abroad. However, it may also involve diaries, video evidence, statements by volunteers investigating the spending of funds abroad and thank you letters from beneficiaries of the charitable funds. All of these can be used to show that the charity has been maintaining control and direction over the funds as they travel from Canada for spending on activities abroad.

There are four ways in which a charity may consider spending its funds on its charitable activities. The first and most obvious is where the charity conducts its activities by itself. The second is where the charity purchases goods and services by way of contract from a third party, such as purchasing mosquito nets rather than making nets themselves. The third and perhaps most popular way involves an *Agency Agreement,* and the final way involves acting in a joint venture or co-operatively with a group of other partners.

OPERATING THROUGH AN AGENT

In an agency relationship there are generally two parties, the principal and the agent. The agent operates as an arm of the principal in the sense that it cannot do anything without the express permission and direction of the principal. (It follows that, if the agent is sued for an activity conducted on behalf of the principal, the principal will also be liable.) These relationships should be established by an *Agency Agreement* between the parties. A sample *Agency Agreement* can be found at **www.runningacharity.ca.**

Typically, the CRA will require an *Agency Agreement* where the agent is not paid for its role in acting as such. As a result, the agents are usually organizations or people already invested in the outcome that the charity seeks to influence.

A detailed agency agreement should be constructed and followed to the letter. Generally, such agreements allow the agent to suggest to the charity as principal some method by which charitable objectives may be furthered. The charity would then consider the suggestion and, if it decides to proceed, it would have internal documentation approving the suggestion. The charity would then transfer a portion of the funds (if sensible in the circumstances) to a bank account upon which the agent has signing authority. This (generally foreign) account would only contain funds belonging to the principal. The agent would, as part of its suggestion, have provided a potential budget for use in the proposed project, and the charity would expect proof that the funds had been spent on the items included in the proposed budget. If this has been established, the charity may authorize the allocation of a second tranche of funds. This process would continue until the project was finished, if ever.

Where the project involves the purchase of assets or real estate, the principal would be expected to exert control and direction over those assets through the agent. This would involve identifying the assets in such a way that they are known to belong to the Canadian charity and ensuring that they are only used for charitable purposes. Implicit in this assurance is knowledge by the charity regarding the purposes for which they are being used, and the ability to withdraw the resources if they are no longer going to be used for charitable purposes. Ideally, it would also require permission by the charity over their use in a particular circumstance, but of course such an arrangement can be difficult to enforce long-distance.

The agency relationship can be administratively difficult in that there will be a great deal of paperwork passed back and forth between the agent and the principal. To make matters worse, CRA expects the charity to maintain **original** documentation in either English or French. Nonetheless, regardless of the administrative difficulties, the agency relationship is the easiest way in which a charity can maintain control and direction over situations in which it operates in a different locality. In those cases where operating via an agency agreement, or perhaps ownership of property in a foreign country is contrary to the local law, the CRA may be consulted for acceptable alternatives.

OPERATING THROUGH A JOINT VENTURE

Many Canadian organizations have sister groups in other countries. For example, religious groups will often have co-religionists who have established operations in places such as the United States, Europe, the Middle East, or Asia. Those groups may wish to undertake a charitable activity together in some foreign country, for example the Catholics in Canada, the United States and the Netherlands working together to build a school in Africa. In such circumstances, an Agency agreement may be inappropriate because it typically involves the agent operating by itself under the direction of the Canadian principal, whereas working with sister groups would clearly contradict this principle.

In these circumstances the CRA is prepared to accept organizations operating as part of a joint venture. A joint venture exists where different parties all contribute something to the overall project. In these circumstances, the Charities Directorate expects the organization to maintain control and direction over the overall project in proportion to the resources it contributes. For example, in a $1,000,000 project, if a Canadian charity was contributing 30%, the CRA would expect the organization to have 30% representation on the board of management for the project.

In a joint venture relationship, it can often be hard to show control and direction, even with some seat on management. Clearly, if the Canadian charity is only a minority participant it will not be able to call the shots on how the project is developed. The recognition by the CRA of a joint venture is *de facto* recognition of the practical principal that Canadian charities do not operate in a vacuum and they often operate with partner organizations abroad. Notwithstanding this recognition of the facts on the ground, a Canadian charity would be well-advised to ensure that whatever project it engages in is in pursuit of its charitable objects and can only be used to pursue those objects.

CO-OPERATIVE AGREEMENTS

A co-operative agreement is a much rarer form of working with others, but still a possible arrangement. As opposed to a joint venture where all of the co-venturers have a role in the final project, in a co-operative arrangement each party only does their specific role without a view to the entire project. For example, a for-profit restaurant could work with a charity to provide employment for the underemployed disabled. The charity has no role in the restaurant and is not responsible for the gain or loss earned, but it does create a program to recruit appropriate employees and perhaps provide them with training or transportation to and from work.

PURCHASING FROM AN OVERSEAS SUPPLIER

Clearly, the CRA is concerned with how a charity spends its resources. Spending within Canada is fairly easy to document because Canadian financial transactions are sophisticated and it is assumed that the organization would be able to document financial transactions from beginning to end.

The same is not necessarily true in foreign jurisdictions. To begin with, receipts are not necessarily standard business practice around the world. Moreover, those receipts would not necessarily be in English or French. Furthermore, in certain countries cancelled cheques are not made available by banks, and in others purchases by cash are the norm. In all of these circumstances, the charity will still be expected to provide documentary evidence that the money has been used to purchase resources solely to further the organization's charitable purposes.

Obviously, the ability to prove this spending depends on the documents that the charity can obtain from the source. However, even where the charity is unable to maintain standard business documentation, it may be possible to collect the necessary documentary evidence. For example, photographs of the purchased material may be sufficient. Similarly, it may be possible to prove the purchase and distribution of certain materials if there is photographic evidence of the final product. For example, the purchase of building materials may be evident in the construction of a final product. In these circumstances, the CRA may be able to accept the fact that a building exists as proof that purchases to buy building materials were also made, and they would also likely require evidence of local prices for such materials. The Tax Court of Canada has suggested that a notebook detailing the purchases with the signature of the vendor may be sufficient evidence, although relying on this exclusively could be risky.

Operating abroad can be fraught with administrative difficulties for charities, but generally once the organization understands the local milieu in which it is operating, the ability to provide the necessary evidence increases as well.

INTERNATIONAL BRANCHES OF THE SAME ORGANIZATION

Being (mostly) a country of immigrants, Canada is an inviting place for international organizations to set up domestic branches. Such groups often require the Canadian branch to pay some form of dues to the international parent body. However, there are strict limitations on the ability of Canadian organizations to help fund the global operations of the groups in which they participate. This is often not understood by the foreign (usually American) 'parent', which often expects the Canadian organization to pay up some percentage of its revenue as dues to the global operation.

The CRA's general policy in this regard is that as the Canadian charity receives benefits from the parent, the Canadian organization may pay 5% of its total expenditures in the year, or $5000 — whichever is the lesser as dues to the parent. The language that the CRA uses in expressing this policy is equivocal so this should only be considered a rule-of-thumb. Often, both the Canadian and foreign organization find this situation highly unsatisfactory.

The relationship between the Canadian and international group is usually one of mutual benefit. The international organization often provides guidance and support, if not actual resources for use in the Canadian branch's operations. Even if the parent organization does not charge for these resources, it may be worthwhile for the Canadian organization to consider paying for them. While the Canadian organization is restricted to paying no more than fair market value for the assets transferred to it, this is one way the Canadian organization may send money back to its parent organization in a way that meets the expectations of both the parent body and the CRA.

Arrangements such as this are complicated and require a valuation of the goods and services coming to the Canadian organization. This valuation should be done by a trained professional to assure the CRA that no more than fair market value is being spent on the goods and services coming back to the Canadian organization from the charity's foreign parent (or any other party).

10 | GST-HST Issues

For most charities the issue of GST/HST is one-sided, that is, it is an issue of paying the tax rather than collecting it. However, charities can be required to collect the GST/HST just as any other organization. The GST/HST issues for charities can be particularly complicated, even in comparison to the other rules that guide them. Unless an organization has very simple financial transactions it should consult an experienced professional regarding its GST/HST obligations. This chapter outlines some of the more salient features of the GST/HST regime to help you ask the appropriate questions.

Structure of the Act

The Federal government charges GST at 5%. Various provincial governments add their percentage of tax on top of the 5% federal portion. In those provinces in which there is a provincial component, the GST is referred to as the Harmonized Sales Tax i.e. the HST. For the most part, the application of the law is the same to all provinces, with the obvious exception of the rates that are charged. However, there are certain differences, the most important of which relate to the amount of rebate to which different charities are entitled. This is outlined later in the chapter.

The GST/HST is the tax levied on all products sold (unless the Excise Tax Act says otherwise) and is designed to be borne by the final consumer of the particular product. So, consumers pay tax on the things they buy. If they in turn combine the item with others they have bought to refashion it as some other item, they generally charge tax on the product sold. Then, that consumer (now producer) remits to the government the total of the tax charged or the final item, less the tax paid on the inputs.

The end consumer pays the tax on the product purchased but cannot claim any credits from the government. The credit for tax paid on inputs is called the *Input Tax Credit*.

Example:

If Lenny purchases fabric from a fabric store he will have to pay the proper GST/HST rate for that province. If he uses that fabric to make a suit for himself then he pays the final tax. If, on the other hand, Lenny produces a suit *for sale* he will collect the proper GST/HST from his customer, deduct from that the amount that he paid to his supplier, and remit the difference to the government. In this way the burden of the tax lies with the ultimate consumer of the product.

Some items are exempt from tax: the consumer does not pay any tax on the item purchased. However, the seller of an exempt product (called an exempt supply) is not entitled to any *Input Tax Credits* on the item sold. This contrasts with items that are called *zero-rated*. These items in fact have a tax rate of 0% (i.e. there is no charge). This entitles the seller of a zero-rated supply to an *Input Tax Credit* of a normal amount. Items which qualify for either treatment are listed in the *Excise Tax Act*.

Given that many charities sell or produce exempt supplies, Parliament has included a mechanism by which these organizations can receive a rebate (rather than a refund) of a portion of the tax paid. In other words, registered charities can receive back 50% of the GST/HST they pay, whether or not the tax is paid on inputs to produce other products. This is to help offset the tax burden the producers of exempt supplies would otherwise shoulder. Our discussion below is limited to the rebate applicable to charities.

Where a charity is engaged in the sale of items that are "Taxable Supplies" (i.e. neither exempt nor Zero-Rated) and in sufficient quantities, the organization may be required to register for a GST/HST number. If the charity does register for such a number they are required to charge tax for the items sold (those of which are neither Exempt nor Zero Rated). Organizations that do sell taxable items may not claim the 100% input tax credits unless they are registered.

EXEMPT SUPPLIES

As described previously, exempt supplies are those for which there is no tax to be paid. And unlike Zero-Rated supplies, there are no Input Tax Credits available for those inputs required to produce such goods. The list of exempt supplies is included within the *Excise Tax Act* and includes most of the items we have come to expect to be provided by charities.

Some property and services are exempt regardless of who supplies them. For example, childcare services (defined as the primary purpose of which is to provide care and supervision of children 14 years of age and under for periods of less than 24 hours per day) are exempt. Other goods and services are exempt if they are provided by a charity whereas they might not be exempt if provided by other types of organizations.

There is a variety of goods and services that charities provide and are therefore exempt from GST/HST. These include:

- Admissions to places of amusement such as museums, recreational complexes and theaters if the maximum admission charge is less than a dollar.

- Admissions to anything where part of the admission qualifies for a charitable donation receipt for income tax purposes (see split receipting in Chapter 6).

- Most property or services sold basically at cost.

- Most property and services sold during the course of a fundraising activity, unless the property or services is part of a year-long business. Examples include Christmas greeting cards, or chocolate bar drives, but not items sold in a year-long gift shop or subscriptions to a charity magazine.

- Membership in a charity, unless there are significant financial benefits to membership.

- Supplies of food and beverages, or a combination provided to relieve poverty, suffering, or distress of individuals.

Sponsorships

As discussed earlier in this book, sponsorships can be an area in which there is a mixed benefit provided back to the donor. For example, a corporation that provides funding to a charity may be given some form of advertising by the charity to its patrons, and the value of the advertising returned to the donor must be reflected in a reduced income tax receipt for the donation to the donor.

Sponsorships may not be subject to GST/HST tax, depending on the nature and extent of the promotional benefits. If the payment by the sponsor is made primarily (more than 50%) to obtain advertising, then the payment will not be considered as sponsorship but rather a payment for advertising services. However, advertising services are generally exempt from GST/HST when provided by a charity. The general question then is whether the organization is engaged in the Taxable Supply of advertising. If there is any question about this, qualified legal counsel should be retained, as the charity may need to be consistently collecting tax on sponsorships.

ZERO-RATED SUPPLIES

Zero-Rated supplies are items for which the tax rate charged on them is 0%, i.e. no tax is actually paid but the seller of those goods can recoup 100% of the tax it paid in producing the item it sold. For this reason, the designation of supplies as Zero-Rated can be relatively beneficial for the supplier. However, the list of supplies is rather small, and typically includes items such as basic groceries, certain goods when they are exported out of Canada, prescription drugs, supplies of blood and blood derivatives, certain medical devices and the rental of farmland.

CHARITIES ELIGIBLE FOR THE GST/HST REBATE

Generally speaking, registered charities are eligible for a rebate of 50% (technically called the *Public Services Bodies Rebate*) of the federal part of the tax (i.e. the 5% amount). Organizations eligible to claim this rebate should file form GST 66 called the *Application for GST/HST Public Services Bodies' Rebate* or form GST 284 *Application for GST/HST Public Services Bodies' Rebate* (both forms are available on **www.runningacharity.ca**). Charities are also entitled to a rebate on the provincial portion in those provinces that participate in the Harmonized Sales Tax. Charities resident in Ontario qualify for 82% rebate of the provincial HST portion; charities in Nova Scotia, New Brunswick, Newfoundland and Labrador qualify for a 50% rebate of their provincial portion; and in Prince Edward Island the rate is 35% of the provincial portion.

GST / HST is rather complicated and there are other mechanisms that can apply to return amounts paid on inputs or reduce the amount of HST charged, such as the purchase of printed books or where most property is produced for export. Clearly, use of these provisions requires experienced advice.

The rebate forms can be filed either electronically using the CRA's online services through GST/HST Netfile or on paper using the form described above. Charities making a filing using either method should also file the appropriate form for the provincial rebate — the *Provincial Schedule Form RC7066SCH, Provincial Schedule — GST/HST Public Services Bodies' Rebate,* also available on **www.runningacharity.ca**. As the rebate percentages for the provincial part of the HST are different for the participating provinces, charities will have to separately track the federal and provincial portions of HST paid on their eligible expenses. For instructions on completing the rebate application, consult *Guide RC4034*. Since charities are subject to audit by the CRA for their GST matters, they must keep necessary documents for six years after the calendar year to which the rebate relates.

REQUIRED REGISTRATION

Most organizations engaged in the supply of taxable goods and services will have to register for GST/HST. There are, however, minimal sales threshold that they must meet before they *are required* to register (see below). Small suppliers may forego the collection of tax on the goods they sell but they are also not entitled to claim input tax credits on the items purchased to produce those goods.

Given that most Canadians are used to paying tax on the items they purchase, the decision to not charge tax and not collect the Input Tax Credits will generally be based on the administrative difficulty that may exist for organizations in tracking the GST/HST in applying for the refund.

Gross revenue test

Charities may qualify as a small supplier under either of the:

- $250,000 gross revenue test, or

- $50,000 tax supplies test.

A charity only needs to meet *one* of these tests to be a small supplier.

The gross revenue test is a calculation of the gross revenue of the charity in the fiscal period, and the test is calculated on the gross revenue over the previous two fiscal years. In the first fiscal year the charity would not have to register for the GST/HST, but in the second year it *must* register if its gross revenue in the first year is more than $250,000. Or, in the third and ongoing years, if the amount is more than $250,000 in either of the two previous years, then it would have to register. Gross revenue includes income from a business, gifts from donations, grants, and property investment income. But again, no registration would be necessary if the charity is not producing a Taxable Supply.

$50,000 Taxable supplies test

Most supplies produced by a charity are exempt and some are zero-rated. However those products or services that are neither exempt nor zero-rated are by definition taxable (or they fall under another exception). If the charity is engaged in the sale of taxable supplies and in the last four calendar years had revenue exceeding $50,000, or in the current quarter will have more than $50,000 the charity will have to register for the collection of tax. This does not include sales of capital property that might attract GST/HST, such as the one-time sale of real estate.

If the amounts are $50,000 or less, the organization does not have to register but may choose to do so voluntarily, as it would allow it to effectively pass the GST/HST onto its final consumers and not shoulder the burden of tax on the inputs it purchases.

ELIGIBLE AND INELIGIBLE EXPENSES

This section relates to the expenses for which a charity can claim the *Public Services Bodies' Rebate* at the applicable rates. The rebate can only be claimed on eligible expenses, typically, those for which one cannot claim input tax credits or any other rebate, refund or omission. They include:

- general operating and overhead expenses such as rent, utilities and administration expenses.

- reimbursements paid to employees and volunteers engaged in delivering the activities of the charity.

- property and services used, consumed or supplied in producing exempt supplies.

- capital property such as buildings, equipment, medicals, machinery etc used mostly in the delivery of exempt supplies.

Certain expenses are ineligible for the *Public Services Bodies' Rebate*. These types of ineligible expenses include:

- memberships in dining, recreational, sporting clubs.

- property or services acquired primarily for making supplies of residential accommodation, unless that accommodation is provided to certain individuals in the pursuit of charitable activities.

- property or services acquired to be given to an officer, member or employee of the charity unless it falls under a specific type of exemption.

This list is not exhaustive and should be reviewed with qualified legal/financial counsel should the charity find itself filing an application for rebate.

11 | Directors' Responsibilities

One of the most common questions a prudent individual will ask before agreeing to become a director of a charity, is whether or not they could be incurring any personal liability by acting as a director. The general answer to this question is that yes, a director *can* become personally liable for the amounts owed by a charity, but that in practice these risks are manageable and indeed, with one exception, are relatively rare. One way these risks can be managed is with proper director and officer insurance, and charities should explore this as a way to ensure that people will agree to serve as directors.

CORPORATIONS VS. UNINCORPORATED ENTITIES

It is important to understand that a corporation is a separate legal entity, so in most cases the obligations of an **incorporated** charity are its own — *and not those of the directors, officers or members.* This is true whether the entity is incorporated federally or provincially. However, there are circumstances where the liabilities (i.e. amounts owed by the corporation) could become the liabilities of the directors, and other situations where the directors could become liable for their actions as directors.

A distinction must be made between the directors of the corporation and the people that act as officers or members. The directors are the mind and management of the organization, so are usually in a position to cause the corporation to do something wrong or improper. Members exercising their vote do not have the same level of micro-managing power (usually). Officers, however, are often in a position of power (sometimes exercising more day-to-day control than the directors, such as in the case of an executive director), so there are limited situations where they could be lumped in with the directors as assuming liability for their actions.

In most cases, the liability becomes the obligation first of the corporation and only under certain circumstances can it then become the liability of directors. The circumstances vary depending on the nature of the liability. For example, a contractual obligation of a corporation is rarely the obligation of the director unless there has been some sort of underhanded or negligent activity by the director. In other circumstances the government may need to take separate action against the individuals in order that the liability becomes that of the director, rather than of the organization.

Trusts and unincorporated organizations do not have this layer of protection. Here the obligations of the charity are the obligations of the trustees or the managers (or whatever the leaders of an unincorporated organization call themselves). Indeed, there may not even be an opportunity to draw a line between the leaders of an unincorporated organization, and the liabilities *may* attach to everyone involved. As trusts do not have members, the liabilities are only those of the trustees. For example, unremitted source deductions are automatically the obligations of the trustees, and the CRA can take collection action against them immediately without first attacking the trust.

TYPES OF LIABILITIES

While ultimately a director may take little comfort in the fact that there are liabilities of different kinds, the fact that they can be divided into categories can be helpful in ensuring that a director meets his or her responsibilities. The divisions are based on whether the actions causing the liability are defined in the common law or by statute. The term common law refers to judge-made law. Over the years, judges have had to define the limits of how the concept of separate corporate personality could protect the directors from personal liability. These limits are generally defined in terms of director's duties, and breaching them leads to liability.

Various laws also assign liability to the directors. For example, environmental acts across the provinces require that an organization maintain the environmental integrity of its property. Failure to do so could result in the directors becoming personally responsible for the damage to the environment, and whatever fines and penalties are levied. These types of penalties against directors make sense, because obviously a corporation is a fictitious legal entity and it is the directors that are the mind and management behind it. As the corporation can really not decide for itself, it is the directors that must bear the responsibility for malfeasance. As a result, there are numerous acts that impose penalties, at least in theory, upon the directors. These include the *Income Tax Act*, the *Excise Tax Act* (HST), Employment laws, the corporate statutes and the *Criminal Code*.

LEVEL OF CARE

One of the advantages of having a board of directors with varied experiences and expertise is to benefit from the multitude of viewpoints. In these circumstances, the group will tend to rely on a director with greater experience in a particular area and look to them to suggest a decision to which the others can reasonably defer. For example, a trained accountant should be better able to find abnormalities in the finances than a college student, and the student will likely rely on the accountant to identify a problem. If the decision made by the directors as a board (but really by the accountant) proves to be one which creates personal liability, a judge must ask if all the directors properly discharged their duties as directors. It would be natural to expect more from the more sophisticated individual than the one with less experience.

The real question then is whether a person is held to some objective standard — usually understood as that of the reasonably prudent person, or whether a Court would compare the actions of the director to a hypothetical person with the same level of understanding, education and sophistication as the individual in question.

Indeed, there is an even higher standard — that of the fiduciary. A fiduciary is someone in a position of trust over the property of another, carrying an obligation to act honestly, in good faith and in the best interests of the other person (in this case the charity) even at the expense of acting in a self-serving manner.

The standard to which an individual is held changes based on the laws and the province. But in a sense, this hardly matters; it would be a poor director indeed who simply did the minimum required and avoided acting in the best interests of the charity. The standard of care is a retroactive test which a judge would use to determine if a director was liable for his actions. Directors would be best advised to, in all circumstances, act diligently — seek out the relevant information, obtain the research necessary to evaluate that information, and always act in the best interests of the charity.

As a general rule, acting diligently and in the best interests of the corporation will meet the standard expected. Rarely can a Court find that a director who has provided a considered and well-informed opinion or worked for the Corporation to meet its obligations was derelict in the responsibility of a director to do their best. Although there are times where there are competing obligations without enough resources to go around, in these cases directors might best exercise their obligations by seeking proper advice.

EVIDENCE

Acting diligently might not make a difference if there is no proof the director did so, so directors should create and retain sufficient evidence that they acted to the best of their ability, honestly and in the best interests of the charity. This can often be in the form of corporate minutes of meetings which record the discussion and the examination of the issue by the directors. It could also be important to keep records of email discussions and any other evidence when the director acts in furtherance of his or her duties. Indeed, it is especially important that an individual director who dissents from the opinion of the majority of the directors to proceed in a certain course of action be recorded in the official minutes. In that way, the dissenting director can always use the record as proof that they had done so.

COMMON LAW DUTIES

Over time, judges have had the opportunity to evaluate the behaviour of both directors of corporations and those in charge of charitable property. In determining whether

these people measured up, the judges first had to outline and define the duties of
these people in fulfilling their roles. These duties became known as the common
law responsibilities, and even if later codified in statute, the comments of judges are
relevant in fully understanding the depth of the responsibility. Over the years, judges
have opined on a number of cases (generally not in Canada, and therefore not prec-
edential but certainly influential). These decisions have used different words for the
same duties and, depending on how they are read, can dramatically expand the list
of responsibilities. However, the responsibilities of directors can be boiled down to
certain commonly accepted principles.

1. Duty of honesty, good faith and loyalty to their charity;

2. Duty to be reasonable, prudent and judicious;

3. Duty to avoid conflict-of-interest situations;

4. Duty to act gratuitously;

5. Duty to account; and

6. Duty to continue.

Most of these duties are self- explanatory and boil down to the responsibility to act
in the best interests of the corporation — to the best of the director's ability even over
the best interests of anybody else and to do so without charge. Clearly, a measure of
an individual's ability to do their best is a subjective judgement, but it is much more
obvious if the director is benefitting from the property of the charity or in a conflict of
interest. From a practical perspective then a charity/director can put in place policies
to ensure that directors are not paid by the charity[19] and always declare any conflicts.

The last two duties are a bit more difficult to understand. The duty to account refers
to the responsibility to keep proper books and records of charitable property. One of the
most fundamental responsibilities of directors is to ensure that charitable property is
properly used, and this cannot happen if the property is not tracked and accounted for.

The duty to continue refers to the director's responsibility to ensure that there is
a constant watch over charitable property. A director cannot simply resign and walk
away from the charity, leaving a vacuum over management of the charitable property.

The enforcement of these duties does not fall within the CRA's jurisdiction, and
technically it is part of the provincial Attorney General's mandate. Unfortunately, other
than Ontario, there is no government office that is tasked with protecting charitable
property. And even in Ontario the Office of the Public Guardian and Trustee rarely
gets involved in reviewing the role directors play in managing a charity. So, while
these duties are the law and are clearly important, there is very little recent precedent
or danger in the director facing consequences for their breach.

---

[19] This extends as far as being paid for services rendered to the charity in some other capacity — so for
example, a painter who is also a director of the charity cannot be paid for services rendered painting
for the charity.

FIDUCIARY OBLIGATIONS

One area in which directors may wish to exercise caution is in their stewardship of funds and donations to the charity for a specific purpose. As an example, imagine a donor who makes a gift — subject to a written deed of gift — that states explicitly the gift must be used to further a project, but the directors then decide to invest the gift, and lose the entire amount. In these circumstances, the directors could be personally liable for misuse of the property. And the danger of enforcement of the pledge is greater because there is an actual donor who exists to enforce the terms of the pledge.

STATUTORY DUTIES

Income Tax Act

Every worker in the country knows that a certain portion of their paycheque is withheld by their employer. At the end of the year, the individual receives a T4 slip with a statement of their gross pay, the amount they actually received and how much was withheld by the employer on account of tax, EI and CPP (there may be other deductions as well for things such as union dues, RRSP contributions or QPP). Once the amounts are withheld by the employer, the worker's obligation to pay tax is met. However, it is then the employer's responsibility to remit those withholdings to the government.[20] Where the employer does not do so, the CRA will assess penalties and interest on these amounts. If the amounts are still left unpaid, the CRA may try to collect from the assets of the corporation and they may pursue the difference from the directors of the charity. This is known as a director's liability assessment.

There are three defenses for a director against such liability. The first is that the individual director was diligent in trying to ensure that the corporation remitted its tax. This is a matter of evidence and circumstance. Without evidence to indicate to the CRA that individual was diligent, the director will not succeed in showing that they should not be liable. Keep in mind the onus to prove this is on the director and not on the CRA. It is also a matter of circumstance, as what it requires to be diligent may change depending on the situation. For example, if the funds are sitting in a bank account and one individual with control over the bank account simply refuses to make the remittances, the other directors may have to seek that individual's removal as a signing officer in order to show diligence. In another circumstance, the directors may want to show that they sought to fund raise to pay the liability owing by the charity. One cannot say for certain in advance what would meet this standard of diligence, but clearly without evidence of any diligence the directors would fail.

Another defense is that the individual ceased being a director two years before the

---

[20] It is beyond the scope of this book to discuss whether an individual is an employee or a contractor. However, it is worth noting that many employers have found out after the fact that should have been withholding tax and remitting it to the government. Caution should be exercised in determining whether an individual is an employee or contractor.

CRA attempted to assess the individual for the liability of the corporation. This is an important rule and it is up to the director to prove that they ceased being a director over two years ago. Again, there must be evidence of this fact. As discussed earlier in this book, corporations must file an annual corporate return every year which lists its directors. This listing is publicly available and the CRA will use it to identify and contact directors, but it does not legally affect an election or removal of directors. For that, the individual director must make sure that when their term is completed or they resign as a director, the proper legal mechanics are observed to make sure that the clock starts running. It is also wise to make sure that the corporate filing is correct and the CRA knows when a person is no longer a director.

The final defense, not counting technical deficiencies with the CRA's actions or bankruptcy, is to ensure that there is proper insurance in place to meet any income tax obligations. While directors and officers insurance should be undertaken by every charity, we have seen policies that, surprisingly to us, even covered unpaid taxes. To our mind if such a generous policy is available, it should be put in place by the charity.

It is important to understand, that the obligations of the directors are not divided amongst them, they are *all* responsible for *all* of the unremitted source deductions. This means that if the CRA were to pursue one wealthy individual, that individual could not argue that she should only be responsible for a pro-rata share of the amount owing. Rather, if they were assessed by the CRA, each director would be entirely responsible for the full amount found owing, and it would be up to them to distribute the debt between them.

Taking action

One way that directors may be able to protect themselves is to insist upon a report from the executive director of the charity at each meeting — along with proof — that the tax and payroll obligations of the organization are met. This would at least serve to show that the directors were diligent in ensuring the obligations were being paid, and if there was a problem, they could take early steps either to correct the problem or to remove themselves as directors.

Income Tax Act civil penalties

The *Income Tax Act* contains a provision designed to ensure that those people who provide tax advice or documentation to others do so with a certain level of care that the individual's tax obligations are being met. For charities, this typically means that the tax receipt must be correct in both form and substance.

An individual who does not exercise the proper care to ensure that the tax obligations of the recipient of the receipt are met could be guilty of culpable conduct. The penalty for such conduct is to pay 50% of the understated tax created by (in this case) the incorrect receipt. In theory, the CRA could asses each director, and the organization, along with any employees or advisors who engaged in "culpable conduct" in issuing false receipts, and each could be responsible for the full amount of the penalty. In these cases, even a director that did not know *but should have known* that this was going on may be responsible.

There have been several cases where the CRA has, in fact, assessed these penalties against officials of charities. Typically, these were in situations where the charities were involved in tax shelter arrangements that the CRA found to be overly aggressive and resulted in the charity issuing improper receipts, but it is entirely possible that the CRA could use these provisions to attack charity directors and charities more broadly. It is incumbent upon the directors to seek legal advice and to maintain constant vigilance regarding the issuance of the charitable receipts. If the directors ever feel that the advice that they have received has been incorrect, they should seek out a second opinion or otherwise act to ensure that the receipts being issued by the charity are entirely above board.

Excise Tax Act

Generally speaking, charities are not responsible for the charging and collection of HST/GST. The situation regarding PST may be different in those provinces that still have that tax. Nevertheless, the fact that charities are not typically required to charge HST/GST does not mean that they never charge these amounts. Indeed, it would be extremely dangerous to rely on the rule-of-thumb that charities typically provide exempt supplies and therefore do not need to charge HST. In circumstances where an organization should charge tax and does not, it becomes liable for the tax and loses the benefit of the Input Tax Credits it may have been able to claim.

The CRA considers amounts of HST/GST to be trust amounts. This is true even if the matter under debate is one where the charity did not charge HST. As a result, the CRA's view is that it can take collection action against the corporation and then against the directors once certain technical requirements are met, even if the charity does not hold any HST.

Taking action

Any time that the charity is selling anything it is important to be certain whether or not there is no requirement to charge HST. Furthermore, given that the law may change from time to time it would be wise to occasionally double check the charity's position. It is amazing how quickly the interest and penalties on 13% of gross sales can mount. The potential liability relating to this is huge and cannot be overlooked.

Other Acts

There are a variety of statues in every province that can impose liability upon directors, and it is beyond the scope of this book to review all of them. Indeed, based on the number of reported decisions, the instances where charity directors are penalized for actions taken while a director are very few. This is not to say that the directors do not bear some risk, but only that, generally speaking, the charities do not expose themselves to this risk, and that the various authorities are seemingly reluctant to pursue directors of charities for these obligations.

Indeed this seems wise, as it is already difficult to encourage experienced directors to serve on the boards of smaller organizations. Charities need all the help they can get in this regard and as long as most of risks can be dealt with through insurance or other means, there is no reason to fear negative consequences from the prudent and considered execution of the director's duties.

PART III

DEATH OF A CHARITY

—

12 | Winding up a Charity

DISSOLUTION: TAX CONSIDERATIONS

Many Canadians who begin a business do not contemplate its possible end, and the same is true of the well-meaning individuals who begin charities. Unfortunately, the death of a charity is at least as common as the death of a business. Often, charities shut down simply because no one is interested in continuing to run them. In other circumstances, the termination of a charity results from the loss of its status as a tax-exempt organization with the CRA. But regardless of the reasons for shutdown, the charity (or more practically, the board of directors) has a number of responsibilities to ensure an orderly windup. If they wish to avoid unnecessary liabilities, directors must fight the temptation to passively allow an inactive charity to languish. A good working knowledge of the rudimentary rules will ensure that neither the charity nor its directors are left exposed upon dissolution.

Perhaps the greatest reason to ensure an orderly windup is that under the *Income Tax Act* a deregistered organization must dispose of its assets in satisfaction of the so-called "revocation tax." Another important motivator for orderly dissolution of a charity is that the fiduciary duties that attach to directors may extend indefinitely if the charity is not carefully terminated.

Of course, any dissolving entity may be left with responsibilities under a variety of different laws, including the *Excise Tax Act*, employment legislation, or the various environmental protection acts. Charities may also be subject to laws that pertain specifically to them as a class, such as Ontario's *Religious Organizations Lands Act* or *Charities Accounting Act*. This chapter will deal primarily with the dissolving charity's responsibilities under the *Income Tax Act*.

CHANGE OF STATUS

As discussed in Chapter 3 an organization is deemed a charity based on whether it has been formed to pursue charitable purposes — regardless of whether or not it is registered as a charity with the CRA. However, registration as a charity clearly has a number of tax advantages and so is pursued by most charities in Canada. The disadvantage of registration is the requirement to abide by the rules imposed on such charities; including those that apply to charitable property should the charity have its registered status revoked.

A registered charity generally loses its status in one of three ways: it voluntarily seeks to have its status revoked; it is revoked for failure to file its annual return; or it is revoked for "serious" non-compliance. According to the CRA, serious non-compliance involves an evaluation of the relative monetary size of the infraction, its criminality, breaches of "major" provisions of the Act, or a breach of a previous compliance agreement.

PROCESS

Regardless of the initiating event, the first legal step in the revocation process — the issuance of a *Notice of Intent to Revoke* by CRA to the charity — is always the same. Revocation begins with this notice, whether the charity requested the revocation or it was initiated by audit. Once the *Notice of Intent to Revoke* (NIR) is issued, legal steps (detailed below) begin and there is a defined process which leads to the finalization of the deregistration of the charity.

As the name implies, the NIR is not the revocation itself, but rather a sign that the CRA intends to proceed to that end. Once the NIR is issued it will only be rescinded if an appeal through the proper process is successful. Despite the importance of the NIR, it can be easy to miss as it is simply a letter (rather than a form) where the "Re" line states the purpose of the letter.

Actual revocation is only effected with publication in the *Canada Gazette;* a federal publication that is used to proclaim the legal effectiveness of certain government acts. The Gazette is the official newspaper of the Canadian government, but hardly anyone outside of government reads it.

Each NIR is dated with the date of *mailing* (i.e. not the date of receipt). This date is important as it is the first day in several timelines. The first is the "winding up" period, the second is the "objection" period, and the third is the date on which the CRA can finalize the revocation with a publication of the notice in the *Canada Gazette.*

Charities can also lose their receipting privileges either temporarily or permanently through suspension or annulment of their privileges by the CRA. In theory, a charity whose receipting privileges are suspended is not in any stage of dissolution, so suspension is not relevant to the present discussion. Annulment, however, can be considered a form of dissolution in that the charity has lost its registered charity status and so it is addressed as well.

VOLUNTARY REVOCATION

Some charities are lucky enough to accomplish the objective that they set out to do and so the need for the charity may evaporate. Other charities may run into difficulties raising the necessary funds to continue effective operation and therefore shut down due to business considerations. Still others may suffer from a lack of volunteers. In all of these cases, the board of directors may make the decision that the time has come to shut down the activity, and where the charity was registered with the CRA, part of the process will involve a voluntary revocation of the charity.

Under most registration systems, if the registrant no longer wishes to be registered they simply remove themselves from the system. The charity registration system is different in that once registered, the CRA retains the sole ability to remove a charity from the list. "Voluntary" revocation refers to the charity's request of the CRA to exercise its authority to deregister the charity.

Revocation can be requested by writing to:
Charities Directorate
Canada Revenue Agency
Ottawa ON
K1A 0L5

The letter to the CRA need not be any particular format but must be signed by an authorized representative of the charity (as defined by the charity's governing documents). Once received, the CRA will send a confirmation letter to the charity and then, in due course, the *Notice of Intent to Revoke* which begins the winding up period.

The organization will then have to follow the same procedures regarding the payment of the revocation tax.

FAILURE TO FILE

Technically, revocation for failure to file is treated similarly to any other type of charitable revocation. Practically speaking, however, this type of revocation is so common that it occupies a special place on the spectrum of reasons for dissolution.

Every registered charity is required to file a yearly information return with the CRA within six months of the end of its fiscal year. Failure to do so is punishable by either a $500 fine or revocation. As a matter of course, charities that fail to file the information return on time receive a reminder notice from the Directorate warning that the charity is in default of filing. If the charity continues in its failure to file, it will receive a *Notice of Intention to Revoke*. However, unlike other causes for revocation, this one has a statutory remedy. A revoked charity can avoid the revocation tax by paying all amounts owing under the either the *Income Tax Act*[21] or the *Excise Tax Act* (although generally there are none in either) and filing all necessary returns under the *Income Tax Act* (which is assured).

---

[21] While it is true that charities are known as tax exempt entities, they are only exempt under Part I of the *Income Tax Act* (which is in fact the largest and most important Part), but it is possible that a charity could be taxable under another part of the *Income Tax Act*.

While this may stop the revocation tax from applying, the charity still needs to be re-registered. To do this, the CRA requires the revoked charity to file a *New Application for Registered Charity Status* (form T1789), which will be considered like any other new application for registration. Thus, the charity bears the risk of being denied registration even though it may have previously been operating as a registered charity, perhaps even for many years. The CRA also applies the controversial practice of requiring the charity to pay an additional $500 for the registration, ostensibly the penalty for missing the filing in the first place.

Technically, a charity could file a *Notice of Objection to an NIR* for failure to file a return but it would be a rare circumstance indeed where a charity could have the revocation withdrawn on such grounds. As such, these types of revocations generally proceed with a re-registration.

REVOCATION FOR CAUSE

The CRA retains the right to revoke a charity's registration for even the slightest infraction of the rules that pertain specifically to charities. (Sometimes, the CRA even tries to argue that a charity should be revoked for infractions for which revocation is not the standard penalty for non-charities — such as improper T4s or unpaid source deductions.) However, the CRA has its own set of guidelines which it uses to determine when revocation may be the appropriate remedy.

Generally speaking, revocation is reserved for the most serious cases of non-compliance. This subjective judgment is made by the CRA at its sole discretion — although CRA officers are theoretically open to discussion before pursuing this course of action.

There are two ways to avoid revocation for cause. The first is to examine the underlying activity and determine whether, factually, the activity in fact transgressed the law. The second is to argue that revocation is an inappropriate remedy based on the CRA's own guidelines. Generally, the first of these methods is argued most effectively by lawyers trained specifically in the area, while the second area may involve appealing to the CRA officer's own sense of a fair result in the circumstances.

Many charities attempt to argue that revocation is inappropriate because the charity does good work. That approach rarely works. By definition, all registered charities have achieved that status because of the good work they do, and the rules apply to all charities equally.

The CRA's guidelines have been previously been published and are available on **www.runningacharity.ca.**

PUBLICATION IN THE GAZETTE

As noted earlier, deregistration is not final until the CRA publishes notice of the revocation in the *Canada Gazette*. Technically, the CRA can publish the notice 30 days after the date of the NIR but it generally refrains from doing so until the charity has had a chance to exercise its rights of appeal to the Charities Redress Section or the courts. This delay can be very useful in planning what can be done to ensure that those the charities help are not left in the lurch should the charity lose its appeal.

There is no legislated wording for the notice, but they are simple statements that the CRA revokes the charitable registration of the organization, listing its formal legal name and business number.

The Gazette comes out every Friday in both electronic and print versions. Both are equally definitive. While anyone can subscribe to the Gazette, it is generally only distributed to courts, law libraries and subscribers.

IMMEDIATE REVOCATION

Under certain circumstances the CRA will not hold itself to a delay in finalizing the revocation and will proceed with publication in the Gazette as soon as possible after 30 days from the NIR has elapsed. The CRA's policy is that it will only pursue this course of action when the charity is engaged in "serious non-compliance."

The potential for abuse by the CRA of this policy is clear, in that a revoked charity is forced to divest itself of its assets and cannot issue receipts to raise funds to pay for its appeal. At first, the CRA limited itself to immediate revocation only against charities that were involved in tax shelters (an area that the CRA worked for a long time to shut down). But the CRA has expanded that program and sought immediate revocation against other charities including churches and even a private school (weeks before the start of the school year).

Immediate revocation of a charity's registration can be fought at the Federal Court of Appeal. There is a three-part test which the Court applies to determine whether it should require the CRA to delay publication. The test looks at the seriousness of the issues involved, whether the harm from a revocation would be irreparable, and the balance of convenience. Notably, the test applied by the Court in determining whether or not immediate revocation should proceed is different than the CRA's test as to whether or not it is warranted.

Obviously, if a charity wishes to fight an immediate revocation it should seek representation by an experienced lawyer.

WHAT IS THE TAX STATUS OF A REVOKED CHARITY?

Revocation obviously leads to the result that the organization in question is no longer a registered charity, but from a tax perspective, if it is not a registered charity then what is it? Clearly, only registered charities can issue charitable donation tax receipts, but the other major question is whether the organization is now taxable on any income it receives as a result of activities or investments.

The answer depends on the nature of the newly-revoked organization and the reasons for revocation. The *Income Tax Act* allows for two possibilities; either the organization is now a not- for-profit, and therefore non-taxable, or it is a for-profit organization and it must pay tax on its income.

A not-for-profit organization is:

> "...a club, society or association that, in the opinion of the Minister, was not a charity within the meaning assigned by subsection 149.1(1) and that was organized and operated exclusively for social welfare, civic improvement, pleasure or recreation or for any other purpose except profit, no part of the income of which was payable to, or was otherwise available for the personal benefit of, any proprietor, member or shareholder thereof unless the proprietor, member or shareholder was a club, society or association the primary purpose and function of which was the promotion of amateur athletics in Canada."[22]

Interestingly, just because a charity is deregistered does not necessarily imply that the CRA no longer believes the organization is a charity at law — just that it ceases to qualify for status. This is most clearly true in the case of revocation for failure to file. So it cannot be taken as a given that a revoked charity is a not-for-profit. Assuming that, in the Minister's opinion, the organization is still a charity, it would not qualify as a not-for-profit and the income of the charity could become taxable.

The categorization as a charity or a not-for-profit is especially germane when the organization is carrying on a for-profit activity. Charities may conduct business with a view to a profit, but not-for-profits cannot. So if a charity is revoked for some reason, (for example the CRA does not believe it really is a charity at law) it cannot necessarily assume that it can still conduct its business activities in a non-taxable manner.

Any revoked charity that seeks to avoid paying tax on its income should consult a lawyer to determine their technical status.

ANNULMENT

Under certain circumstances, the CRA may annul the charitable registration of any charity. This procedure is only available where the CRA believes it originally registered the charity in error, or the law has changed and if the organization were to apply today it would not qualify for status.

Valid receipts issued prior to the annulment remain valid. Moreover, the newly-annulled charity is not subject to the revocation tax. While it at times it may seem that the CRA believes that agreement by the charity is necessary in order to annul its registration, this is not the case and a charity may receive a notice of annulment from the CRA to which it may engage in the objection procedure as described more fully later in this chapter.

---

[22] Paragraph 149(1)(l) of the *Income Tax Act*

PROPERTY IN THE CHARITABLE SPHERE

As a matter of policy, the Act is designed so that once property is donated to a registered Canadian charity it will stay within the charitable sector. For example, the Act allows the transfer of receipted property from the recipient charity to another "qualified donee" as that term is defined in the *Income Tax Act*. Consistent with this philosophy, the Act allows for the payment of the so-called "revocation tax" to certain "eligible donees" other than the tax man.

REVOCATION TAX

If the CRA issues a *Notice of Intent to Revoke*, the charity becomes liable to pay a tax effectively equal to the fair market value of its assets on the date of the *Notice of Intention to Revoke* less its debts. The CRA summarizes the calculation as follows:

> The revocation tax is the total value of all remaining assets after all debts and liabilities have been paid. Specifically, it is the total of the following calculation:
>
> - the fair market value of the charity's property on Day 1;
> - any appropriations that occurred in the 120 day period ending on Day 1; and
> - the income received during the winding-up period.
>
> Less
>
> - any expenditures (including amounts spent on charitable activities) during the winding-up period;
> - any debts the charity owes on Day 1; and
> - any property transferred to an eligible donee during the winding-up period.
>
> **Day 1** is the day after the *Notice of Intent to Revoke* and the winding up period is:
>
> - the day on which the charity files Form T2046, *Tax Return Where Registration of a Charity is Revoked*, but no later than the day on which the charity is required to file that return;
> - the day on which the Minister last issues a notice of assessment of revocation tax payable under the Act for that taxation year by the charity; and
> - if the charity has filed a *Notice of Objection* or appeal in respect of that assessment, the day on which the Minister may take a collection action under the Act in respect of the tax payable.

Even after the charity's revocation is confirmed, the resolution of an objection to an assessment of revocation tax could itself take several years. The major reason a charity would consider filing a *Notice of Objection* in such circumstances would be to dispute the value of the charity's assets where the CRA believes more is owing and is attempting to extract payment of this alleged excess.

THE WINDING-UP PERIOD

The first time period in which the organization must calculate its revocation tax ends on the date the (now revoked) charity received the *Notice of Intent to Revoke*. The second time period is defined by the Act as the winding-up period of the charity. This period begins on the day *after* the *Notice of Intent to Revoke*, and ends on the latest of three possible dates:

- The day on which the charity files the appropriate returns as described below;

- The day on which the Minister issues a *Notice of Assessment* for the revocation tax; or

- If the charity has filed a notice of objection or appeal in respect of that assessment, the day on which the Minister may take a collection action.

While the winding-up period does not technically include the time period during which the charity objects to and/or appeals the *Notice of Intent to Revoke*, practically speaking the CRA will not issue a notice of assessment of tax until it is determined with certainty that the charity's registration is actually revoked. In fact, the CRA's *RC4424 Guide to Completing the T2046* states explicitly that where a charity objects to the original *Notice of Intent to Revoke*, the CRA will extend the "revocation period" (presumably they mean the winding-up period) to three months *after* all rights of appeal have been exhausted.

During this winding-up period, the charity has no receipting privileges and may or may not be a not-for-profit entity. Nevertheless, any income earned by the organization during the winding-up period (including gifts) becomes eligible for the revocation tax. Additionally, certain non-arm's length individuals — such as directors — who receive assets of the charity for less than their fair market value during the winding-up period become liable for the payment of the revocation tax.

A revoked charity may deduct from the assets eligible for the revocation tax anything it spent on charitable activities during the winding-up period. Of course, given that a charity may have its registration revoked due to the CRA disagreeing that its charitable activities are in fact charitable, it can be difficult to make spending decisions, and this in itself can lead to a new avenue of dispute.

ELIGIBLE DONEES

As previously outlined, a charity can deduct from the revocation tax payable to the government any payments made to an "eligible donee" during the winding-up period. From a policy perspective, this is consistent with the overall scheme to keep charitable assets in the sector rather than paid to the government. Of course, there is the added benefit that the federal government does not want to be seen seizing the assets of orphanages and schools.

There is a difference between an eligible donee and a qualified donee.

An eligible donee:

- Has 50% or more of its directors dealing at arm's length with the directors of the revoked charity;

- Does not have its registered charity status suspended;

- Has no unpaid liabilities under either the *Income Tax Act* or the Excise Tax Act;

- Has filed all information returns required by the *Income Tax Act*; and

- Is not the subject of a certificate issued under the *Charities Registration (Security Information) Act* or, if it is, the certificate has been determined not to be reasonable.

- Certain municipalities approved by the CRA on a case by case basis.

By comparison, a qualified donee includes:

- Registered charities;

- RCAAAs;

- Certain housing corporations;

- Municipal or public bodies forming a function of government in Canada;

- The United Nations or any of its agencies;

- Certain prescribed universities outside of Canada;

- Certain organizations outside of Canada that have received gifts from the Canadian government; and

- The Crown in right of Canada or a province.

RETURNS UNDER THE *INCOME TAX ACT*

A revoked charity must file with the Minister a form T2046 — *Tax Return Where Registration of a Charity is Revoked* and the usual T3010A for the period from the start of the fiscal year to the date of the NIR. If the revoked charity fails to file a T2046, the CRA will issue a notice of assessment for revocation tax based on the latest numbers available to the CRA either from the last filed T3010 or audit. It is worthwhile to note that the revoked charity owes this amount as soon as the notice of assessment is issued.

The T2046 form is a technical document, and it could lead to a dispute over revocation tax. It is best filled out by an accountant or other professional individual with knowledge of the organization's finances.

NOTICES OF OBJECTION

If the charity disagrees with the amount of the assessment, it may file a *Notice of Objection* within 90 days of the date on the *Notice of Assessment*. The usual circumstance in which a revoked charity might do this is when the CRA has assessed the wrong amount. If the CRA is unaware of the more recent financial circumstances of the charity, such that the value of the assets has declined since the latest T3010, or were disbursed in the course of charitable activities, or were transferred to an appropriate party, the assessment will be incorrect. Consequently, the revoked charity will either have to file a *Notice of Objection* or pay an assessment for funds it no longer has.

While a *Notice of Objection* for a private taxpayer is sent to the Chief of Appeals at the various Tax Services Offices, it should be noted that a *Notice of Objection* to either a *Notice of Intent to Revoke* or a *Notice of Assessment* against a charity is sent to the:

Assistant Commissioner
Appeals Branch
250 Albert Street, 13th Floor
Ottawa ON
K1A 0L5

It is important to note that unless the charity is not incorporated, or the directors have misappropriated the charity's assets, the assessment for tax will only be against the organization and not the individuals running the charity.

OTHER IMPLICATIONS OF REVOCATION

With the possible exception of charities whose registration is annulled because of a change to the law, the fact that a charity is no longer registered with the CRA does not necessarily mean that the common law applying to charities no longer applies to it. In particular, the fiduciary duties that attach to specified gifts must be kept in mind when disbursing all of a charity's assets. At all times, the terms of the specified gifts should be adhered to (whether by a new charity or an eligible donee that accepts upon itself those obligations). If the terms can no longer be met, the organization may have to apply to the court under the *Cy-Près* doctrine for guidance.

Appendix:
Current Model Objects

Relief of poverty

To relieve poverty by operating a food bank for [specify eligible beneficiaries, for example, individuals or families who are poor, of low income, or in need].

To relieve poverty by operating a soup kitchen for [specify eligible beneficiaries, for example, individuals or families who are poor, of low income, or in need].

To relieve poverty by providing basic necessities of life, including food, clean water, clothing, and/or shelter to [specify eligible beneficiaries, for example, individuals or families who are poor, of low income, or in need].

To relieve poverty by providing food and other basic necessities of life to [specify eligible beneficiaries, for example, individuals or families who are poor, of low income, or in need].

To relieve poverty by establishing, operating and maintaining shelters for the homeless.

To relieve poverty by providing residential accommodation below market rate, support, and incidental facilities to [specify eligible beneficiaries, for example, individuals or families who are poor, of low income, or in need].

Relief of poverty — Developing nations

To relieve poverty in developing nations by providing food and other basic necessities of life to individuals or families in need.

To relieve poverty in developing nations by providing basic necessities of life, including food, clean water, clothing, and/or shelter to [specify eligible beneficiaries, for example, individuals or families who are poor, of low income, or in need].

Relief of poverty – Disaster relief

To relieve poverty by providing necessities of life, including food, clean water, medical supplies, clothing, and/or shelter to victims of disasters.

Advancement of education

To advance education by establishing and operating a public [primary, secondary, or post-secondary] school for [specify eligible beneficiaries] [if required, specify topic(s)].

To advance education by providing books, equipment, and educational aids to students attending [specify name of school].

To advance education by providing classes on the subjects of childbirth education, preparation for parenting, and nutrition to [specify].

To advance education by providing leadership training programs to [specify eligible beneficiary group].

To advance education by providing publicly available scholarships, bursaries, and other forms of financial assistance to [specify eligible beneficiaries] to be used for [specify, elementary, secondary, or postsecondary] education.

To advance education by providing awards to [specify eligible beneficiaries] to encourage academic excellence.

To advance education by training police officers, teachers, social workers, and crisis response workers to recognize and respond to online sexual exploitation and to assist children and youth affected by this issue.

To advance education by operating a science fair for students across Canada.

Advancement of education — Arts

To advance education by providing instructional seminars on topics related to the performing and visual arts to [specify eligible beneficiaries].

Advancement of religion

To advance religion by teaching the religious tenets, doctrines, and observances associated with [specify religion or faith].

To advance religion by preaching the teachings, and religious tenets, doctrines and observances, associated with [specify faith or religion].

To advance religion by establishing and maintaining a house of worship with services conducted (or held) in accordance with the tenets and doctrines of [specify faith or religion].

To advance religion by establishing and maintaining a religious school of instruction on the subject of [specify faith or religion] for [specify children, youths, and/or adults].

To advance religion by establishing a facility to be used for religious programs, workshops, music, and [specify for example Bible, Qur'anic, Talmudic or other] studies.

Other purposes that are beneficial to the community in a way the law considers charitable.

Promotion of health

To promote health by providing the public with [specify type of] medical services.

To promote health by providing affected populations with health care services or products that prevent and manage serious threats to health and survival.

To promote health by providing accident victims with physical, occupational, or speech therapy.

To promote health by protecting and maintaining public health through the operation of a healthy-heart program to slow the development and progression of heart disease.

To promote health by providing individuals with [specify health condition] with access to related counselling, information, or group support programs.

To promote health by providing public ambulance, paramedic, or firefighting services.

Advancing the public's appreciation of the arts

To advance the public's appreciation of the arts by providing high-quality artistic performances in [specify for example, public places, senior citizens homes, churches, community centres, and educational institutions].

To advance the public's appreciation of the arts by producing public art exhibitions, presentations, and performance art(s) events, and by providing a forum for qualified artists to exhibit, present, or perform their artistic works through participation in such events.

To advance the public's appreciation of the arts by:

- providing high-quality public performances of classical choral works; and
- providing free performances for audiences that may not be able to attend regular performances.

Protection of the environment

Ecosystem preservation.

To protect the environment for the benefit of the public by conserving or restoring ecosystems and biodiversity on a long-term basis.

Pollution reduction

To protect the environment for the benefit of the public by conserving ecosystems through saving, supporting, protecting, or assisting stressed or endangered forms of life (including plant and animal life).

To protect the environment for the benefit of the public by reducing pollution for the benefit of the public by operating a water testing and treatment program at [specify location].

To protect the environment for the benefit of the public by reducing pollution and by cleaning up or remediating polluted [specify air, water, or ground].

Promoting the welfare of animals

To promote the welfare of animals for the benefit of the public by spaying or neutering domestic pets, and/or feral or stray animals.

To promote the welfare of animals for the benefit of the public by:

- rescuing stray, abandoned, abused, or surrendered animals; and
- operating an animal adoption program.

Addressing and preventing specific problems faced by children or youth

To address and prevent problems faced by children or youth by providing publicly available crisis counselling.

To address and prevent problems faced by children by operating a latchkey program for [specify eligible beneficiaries, for example, children attending public elementary schools].

To address and prevent problems faced by youth by operating a supervised youth centre (or drop-in centre) that provides structured programs directed toward resolving [specify the problem(s)].

To address and prevent problems faced by youth by establishing, operating, and maintaining a long-term group home for youth dealing with [specify problem(s)].

To address and prevent problems faced by youth by establishing, operating, and maintaining a life-skills learning centre for Aboriginal children and youth dealing with [specify problem(s)].

Addressing and preventing specific problems faced by families

To address and prevent specific problems faced by families by establishing and operating an assessment and counselling center for children, youth, and parents dealing with behaviour management issues.

To address and prevent specific problems faced by families by providing parents, children, and youth with mentoring programs, workshops, and seminars on issues such as anger management, conflict resolution, and effective communication.

To address and prevent specific problems faced by families by providing grief support and counselling for survivors that addresses issues associated with the loss of family members.

To address and prevent specific problems faced by families by providing counselling and outreach programs to individuals affected by family violence.

Relieving conditions associated with the aged

To relieve conditions associated with the aged by providing specially adapted residential accommodation, incidental facilities, and support to [specify eligible beneficiaries].

To relieve conditions associated with the aged by providing personal care, housekeeping, meals, nursing, shopping assistance, and transportation to medical appointments to [specify eligible beneficiaries].

Relieving conditions associated with disability

To relieve conditions associated with disability by providing specially adapted residential accommodation, incidental facilities, and support to [specify eligible beneficiaries].

To relieve conditions associated with disability by providing trained personnel and specialized services that assist [specify eligible beneficiaries] in their daily activities.

To relieve conditions associated with disability by providing athletic and recreational programs to support the physical, mental, and emotional well-being of [specify eligible beneficiaries].

To relieve conditions associated with disability by providing life management counselling and other supportive services to [specify eligible beneficiaries] to become and remain more independent in the community.

To relieve conditions associated with disability by providing job training and job placement assistance to [specify eligible beneficiaries].

To relieve conditions associated with disability by providing camps with specially adapted programs and facilities for children or youth with [specify condition(s)].

To relieve conditions associated with disability by providing assistive devices to [specify eligible beneficiaries].

Providing public amenities

To provide a public amenity by establishing and maintaining a memorial garden for the public.

To provide a public amenity by establishing and maintaining a park in [specify community].

To provide a public amenity by establishing and maintaining a public children's playground].

To provide a public amenity by establishing, administering, and maintaining a multi-use recreational facility in [specify community].

To provide a public amenity by establishing and maintaining a [specify type of museum] for the public.

Protecting and preserving significant heritage sites

To protect and preserve significant heritage sites by restoring, developing, and maintaining the [specify the historic site] with a view to commemorating the site and educating the public about it.

Promoting the efficiency of the Canadian Armed Forces

To promote the efficiency of the Canadian Armed Forces for the benefit of the public by providing [air, sea, or army] cadet training to youth.

Promoting commerce or industry

To promote and maintain efficiency and high standards of practice in the [specify industry, trade, or profession] for the benefit of the public by developing training programs for, and providing funds for the training of, individuals engaged in the [industry, trade or profession].

To promote excellence and efficiencies in the [specify industry, trade or profession] in Canada for the benefit of the public by establishing and maintaining best practices and standards of workmanship, through the development and institution of an apprenticeship program.

To promote excellence in the [specify industry, trade or profession] in Canada for the benefit of the public by conducting research on best practices related to that [specify industry, trade or profession] and disseminating the results of the research to the public.

Gifting to qualified donees

Ontario:

To receive and maintain a fund or funds and to apply all or part of the principal and income therefrom, from time to time, to charitable organizations that are also registered charities under the *Income Tax Act* (Canada).

For all other Canadian jurisdictions:

To receive and maintain a fund or funds and to apply all or part of the principal and income therefrom, from time to time, to qualified donees as defined in subsection 149.1(1) of the *Income Tax Act* (Canada).

Glossary

A

Amalgamation The process of legally merging two corporations into one.

Association Technically an unincorporated group of individuals who come together in pursuit of a common cause but may also be used in the name of a charity.

B

Brackets In a tax sense referring to a range of income between a lower and higher threshold. A different tax percentage is applied to each bracket.

Business number The number assigned to each entity, business or not, by the CRA.

C

Canada Gazette A publication of the Government giving formal notice of, amongst other things, the revocation of a charity's registration.

Canada Not-for-profit Corporations Act (**also the "CNCA"**) The law by which corporations without share capital are legally constituted federally.

Capital The holdings of an organization as opposed to its income in a year. Also, the amount of an investment to generally earn income.

Charitable objects The purposes for which a group is organized and must conform to the legal understanding of charity.

Charitable organization As distinct from a foundation. Generally, a registered charity that acts to pursue its objects, rather than distribute funds to other organizations.

Charities Registration (Security Information) Act A law designed to monitor and immediately revoke the registration of charities engaged in terrorist activities.

Charity registration The process by which the CRA confirms that an entity is subject to the advantages and disadvantages of being a charity under the *Income Tax Act*.

Common law Law that applies by virtue of judicial decision rather than statute

Constitution The document intended to provide rules for which an unincorporated group of people may work together.

Co-operative agreement An agreement between one or more organizations to each pursue their own projects with the intention that the projects benefit each other.

Corporation The artificial legal construct which exists as a legal person separate from its members or directors.

D

Deed of Gift A legal document signifying the transfer by of gift from the owner of property to another.

Directors The people who are elected into the position of being the mind and management of the organization.

Disbursement quota The amount that a charity must expend in a year from its assets not otherwise used in charitable activities.

Dissolution clause The statement in an organization's constituting documents, stating how its assets will be distributed one dissolution.

Donation tax credit The amount by which tax owing is reduced by virtue of a receipted donation to a qualified donee.

Donations/Gift Property ownership legally transferred from a legal owner to another entity with no expectation of return.

E

Eligible donees The group of entities to which a revoked charity may transfer its assets.

Endowment Generally, an invested amount of capital invested by a charity.

Excess business holding rules The laws which restrict a private foundation from holding shares of a business.

Excise Tax Act The law regarding GST and HST.

Exempt supplies A product for which HST is not charged and for which Input Tax Credits can not be claimed.

F

Fair market value The determination of the value an item would fetch in an open and relevant market.

Fiduciary Describes the position of trust one individual may have over another. Usually denotes the highest level of legal and ethical responsibility.

G

Gift *See* **donation**.

Gifting arrangement A technical term for a tax shelter which involves donation to charity.

H

Heads of charity The broad categories of charity which include relief of poverty, the advancement of education, the advancement of religion and other purposes which the law has determined are beneficial to the community.

I

Income Generally, all forms of value which accrue to an entity within the year.

Income Tax Act The law regulating the taxation of income and the regulation of charities.

Input Tax Credit The HST paid on an input used to produce a final item which is credited towards the HST remitted to the government on the sale of the final item.

ITA See *Income Tax Act*.

J

Joint venture An operation between two or more entities who work together in pursuit of a singular objective.

L

Liabilities The amounts owed by one entity to another.

M

Members In a corporate sense, the individuals responsible for electing the directors but are specifically defined in the relevant law and corporate bylaws.

N

Non-qualifying securities As defined in the *Income Tax Act,* generally securities that are not publicly traded on a recognized exchange.

Not-for-profit As defined in law, an organization that meets the legal definition but is neither a registered charity nor a for-profit organization.

Notice of Assessment A legal document sent by the CRA effectively invoicing the recipient for amounts of tax owed.

Notice of Intent to Revoke A document sent by the CRA indicating that it will proceed with final revocation of the charity's registration.

Notice of Objection A document filed by a taxpayer or charity to either a notice of assessment or a notice of intent to revoke stating the author's wish to appeal the CRA's position.

Notice of Refusal to Register A notice by the CRA that it will not give registered charitable status to an applicant.

O

Officer A position in a corporation that is defined by law, bylaw or resolution that is not a member or director and generally deals with the day to day work of the corporation.

P

Partisan political activities Generally, activities in support of one or more political actors or positions to the exclusion of others.

Private foundation As defined in law, an organization that receives most of its funds and is controlled by not arm's length people.

Public benefit The requirement that a charity aims to provide salutary effects to a significantly large group of people.

Public foundation An entity which is controlled by non-arm's length people and receives funds from the public but generally uses them to distribute to other qualified donees.

Public Service Bodies' Rebate The calculation of HST paid by registered charities and others that is returned to those organizations.

Publicly-traded corporations Entities whose shares are bought and sold on stock exchanges.

Q

Qualified donees The list of entities in the *Income Tax Act* that are treated similarly for donation purposes to registered charities.

R

RCAAAs Registered Canadian Amateur Athletic Associations — entities which have a status similar to registered charities which are designed to promote amateur athletics across the country and meet other qualifications.

Related business The for-profit business activity of a charity that is related to its objects and subordinate to them.

Revocation tax The amount of tax owing by a deregistered charity.

RRSP The tax-free accumulation of income for the purposes of retirement as allowed by law.

S

Soliciting corporations As defined by the CNCA, a corporation which receives more than $10,000 by way of solicitation from public sources.

Source deductions The amount of an individual's pay entitlement withheld by the employer for remittance to the CRA on the individual's account.

Statute of Elizabeth Also known as the Statute of Uses, the preamble of which is the source of charity law in Canada.

Strike price The amount at which stock in a corporation may be purchased by the owner of the option.

T

Tax credit An amount that reduces tax owing.

Tax deduction An amount that reduces the taxable income upon which tax is calculated.

Taxable income As defined by the *Income Tax Act* is gross income less applicable deductions.

Trust Is a relationship between the legal owner of property and those entitled to benefit from it or the legal owner of property and the purposes for which it must be used.

Trustees The legal owners of property who are not also entitled to benefit from the property.

U

Unincorporated association See **association**.

V

Voluntary revocation The act of a charity willingly giving up its charitable registration.

W

Will A document written by an individual which details how they wish for their assets to be distributed upon death.

Winding-up period The period that begins the day after the Notice of Intent to Revoke and ends on the date determined by law or CRA policy.

Z

Zero rated Items for which the HST tax rate is zero percent, entitling the producer to claim Input Tax Credits.

Index

www.ingramcontent.com/pod-product-compliance
Lightning Source LLC
Chambersburg PA
CBHW081524220326

41598CB00036B/6328